C000148325

1 MONTH OF
FREE
READING

at

www.ForgottenBooks.com

By purchasing this book you are eligible for one month membership to ForgottenBooks.com, giving you unlimited access to our entire collection of over 1,000,000 titles via our web site and mobile apps.

To claim your free month visit:

www.forgottenbooks.com/free512492

* Offer is valid for 45 days from date of purchase. Terms and conditions apply.

ISBN 978-0-428-82491-4
PIBN 10512492

This book is a reproduction of an important historical work. Forgotten Books uses
state-of-the-art technology to digitally reconstruct the work, preserving the original format
whilst repairing imperfections present in the aged copy. In rare cases, an imperfection in
the original, such as a blemish or missing page, may be replicated in our edition. We do,
however, repair the vast majority of imperfections successfully; any imperfections that
remain are intentionally left to preserve the state of such historical works.

Forgotten Books is a registered trademark of FB &c Ltd.
Copyright © 2018 FB &c Ltd.
FB &c Ltd, Dalton House, 60 Windsor Avenue, London, SW19 2RR.
Company number 08720141. Registered in England and Wales.

For support please visit www.forgottenbooks.com

DEMOCRACY UNVEILED;

OR,

TYRANNY

STRIPPED OF THE

GARB OF PATRIOTISM.

BY CHRISTOPHER CAUSTIC, L. L. D.

&c. &c. &c. &c. &c. &c. &c. &c.&c.

——*Cæcum domus scelus omne reterit.*

You *rogues !* you *rogues !* you're all found out
And, " WE THE PEOPLE," I've no doubt,
Will put a period to your dashing,
And *honest men* will come in fashion.

••••••••••••••••••••••••
IN TWO VOLUMES. VOL. II.
••••••••••••••••••••••••

THIRD EDITION, WITH LARGE ADDITIONS.

NEW-YORK :

PRINTED FOR I. RILEY, & CO.
1805.

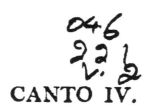

CANTO IV.

𝕮𝖍𝖊 𝕵𝖊𝖋𝖋𝖊𝖗𝖘𝖔𝖓𝖎𝖆𝖉.

ARGUMENT.

With deference due, and huge humility,
Approaching Don Perfectibility,
We laud the man, by Demo's reckon'd
A sort of Jupiter the second, 1
Whose most correct administration
In annals of *Illumination*,
Will ever shine superbly splendid,
A long *time* after *time* is ended.

WITH awe, scarce short of adoration,

Before the glory of our nation,

With scrape submissive, cap in hand,

We, Doctor Caustic trembling stand;

1 A sort of Jupiter the second.

A very judicious encomiast on the " greatest man in America," in an *elegant puff*, published, and republished in almost every democratic Newspaper in the United

2030050

And offer with all veneration
Due to his Highness's high station,
Our services to daub and gloss over
A philanthropical philosopher.

The mighty Chief of Carter's Mountain,
Of democratic power the fountain,
We would extol, his favour buying
By most profound and solid lying.[2]

States, has among other *dashing matters*, drawn a flaming comparison between Messrs. Jefferson and Jupiter.
These two deities seem to share the universe between
them, and to hurl about their thunder and lightning at
an astonishing rate. Perhaps there never was a comparison, which, as rhetoricians express themselves, went
more completely *on all fours*, than this to which we allude. We think, however, that our Mr. Jupiter jun.
whenever he condescends to put on the terrible, is much
the most august of these two personages.

2 By most profound and solid lying.

Butler, speaking, doubtless of a demagogue, says that
he was,

—————————————for profound
And solid lying much renown'd.

A man may *lie* not only with impunity but with ap-
plause, provided his falshoods have a tendency to further

Sure never lucky man of rhyme
Was blest with subject more sublime,
And ere his virtues we've reported,
We shall or ought to be—*transported!*

Touch'd by our pencil, every fault
Shall fade away like mount of salt,
Which late, 'tis said, in weather rainy,
Was melted in Louisiana.[3]

Posterity shall puff the Statesman,
Whom we will prove is our first rate's man,
Nor Gaffer Time shall dare to tarnish
The character we mean to varnish.

But shall we not, as poets use
First set about to seek a muse,

the views of the hypocritical demagogues of the day. See note 12, p. 8. vol. 1.

3 Was melted in Louisiana.

Although we have not yet received *official intelligence* of this most extraordinary phenomenon, yet, the silence which Mr. Jefferson has of late observed on the subject of this stupendous curiosity, warrants the conclusion which we here take the liberty to draw, of its absolute fusion.

One of Apollo's fiddling lasses,
Who runs to grass on Mount Parnassus ?

Dost think we had not better choose
Some mad cap Della Cruscan Muse,
To teach us featly to combine
A world of nonsense in a line ?

Or call on some frail worldly wench,
As did the revolutionary French, [knees on
When th' impious monkies bent their
Before their strumpet-goddess Reason ?4

Or shall we undertake to hire
Some democratic muse, a liar,
Who would, for pelf, in lays most civil,
Sing Hallelujahs to the devil?

4 Before their Strumpet-Goddess Reason?

It is a fact well known to every one in the least con-
versant in the history of the French Revolution, that religious homage, with a great number of blasphemous cer-
emonies was rendered by the chief actors in that scene of
desolation to a common harlot. The object of their adoration was tricked out with characteristic tawdriness, and
personated REASON at that time the idol of those atro-
cious infidels.

Or seek in dark and dirty alley
A Mr. Jefferson's Miss Sally,
In our *Free Government* no matter ⹀
Whether coal black, or swart mulatto ?

No—but with Gallatin's best whisky
OURSELF will get a little frisky,
Then, either foot a poet's stilt on, ʹ
We'll strut away sublime as Milton.

Some say our chief regards religion
No more than wild goose, or a pigeon,
But I'll maintain, what seems an oddity,
He's overstock'd with that commodity.

The man must have religion plenty
To soar from " NO GOD" up to " *twenty*,"
No doubt of common folks the odds
As no God is to twenty Gods.⁵

5 As no God is to twenty Gods.

We have ever greatly admired the wonderful political
pliancy of some of our clerical characters, in supporting
with so much ardour, a man who has ever been
hostile to the christian religion. But these gentlemen no doubt suppose, that the reports of Mr. Jefferson's

Though his high mightiness was skittish,
When menac'd by the bullying British

infidelity are all federal lies. We will however furnish them with a few facts and arguments with which the federalists fortify their assertions, not doubting in the least that these candid and learned divines will contrive to muster arguments to prove, that Mr. Jefferson is a very pious and orthodox sort of a man ; and though perhaps they would not go so far as to assert with a certain itinerant *holder-forth* in Massachusetts, that Mr. Jefferson is the sixth angel mentioned in the revelation, yet, they will probably maintain, that he has as much political piety as Oliver Cromwell, of *genuine* republican memory.

Mr. Jefferson's invitation to Tom Paine, has somewhat the appearance of no great regard to religion. But doubtless it was supposed, that the claims of the latter as a politician were such, as to entitle him to the very extraordinary attention of the former, especially, as Paine had written a letter against General Washington, an opponent to Mr. Jefferson's party, which teemed with the most unqualified abuse.

Mr. Jefferson says, in his Notes on Virginia, " It does me no injury for my neighbour to say, there are twenty Gods, or *no God* ; it neither picks my pocket, nor breaks my leg ; if it be said, his testimony in a court of justice cannot be relied on, reject it then, and be the stigma on him ;" and speaking of the state of religion in Pennsylvania and New-York, he says, " religion there is well supported, of different kinds indeed, *but all good enough ;* all sufficient to preserve peace and order."

The Feds are wrong to make a clatter
About the Carter-Mountain matter.[6]

Now, although federal clergymen might be induced to
adopt the language of Mr. Smith, and exclaim, " which
ought we to be most shocked at, the *levity* or *impiety* of
these remarks?" yet, democratic clergymen will, if they
would be consistent, declare all this to be a federal lie, and
that those passages in the Notes on Virginia which we
have quoted, are federal interpolations, intended to traduce the fair fame of the " greatest man in America."

But there is an astonishing charge lately made by a
writer in the United States Gazette, that demands a
refutation, which we, although the professed eulogist
of Mr. Jefferson, are sorry to confess, are unable to furnish ; but we hope our fellow-labourers in the vineyard of
democracy will supply us weapons, wherewith to knock
down this impudent adversary of our immortal chieftain·
" The most gentle temper," says this anti-Jeffersonian
scribbler, " may be urged until it becomes impatient, and
this, I confess, was the case with myself, when on the
road between Baltimore and Philadelphia, I heard a min-
ister of the gospel declare, that the report of Mr. Jefferson's infidelity was " *a Federal lie.*" To counteract an im-
putation so ungenerous and unjust, and for the information of those, who are not so entirely hoodwinked as not
to see any thing, however obvious and palpable it may
appear, I have thought proper to subjoin the following
statement, and if Mr. Jefferson will deny its truth, he shall
be immediately informed of the name of the person who
made it.

'Twas better far to make excursion,
By way of something like diversion,

" B. Hawkins Esq. (don't start Mr. Jefferson) once a
member of congress, and now high in trust and presidential favour, wrote a pamphlet in vindication of the doc⁻
trines of the Illuminati, and among others, of the doctrines
of *chance* and *materialism.* He sent one copy of this pamphlet, yet in manuscript, to Mr. Jefferson, and another
copy to Mr. Macon, speaker of the house of representatives. I say he sent those copies, and I ask Mr. Jefferson
to deny it.

" Mr. Jefferson, in order to elude the curiosity of the
Post-Office, sent him an answer in LATIN, in which he
has recourse to that unintelligible slang which marks his
public messages, but in which he does *unequivocally* express his approbation of every sentiment contained in the
work, and does request Mr. Hawkins to cause it to be
published, in order to *enlighten the minds of the people of
America.* I say he did send this letter, and I beseech
the President to deny it. The answer of Mr. Macon was
not in latin ; Mr. Macon does not write latin."

This impudent federalist, who thus slanders the chief
magistrate of a christian country, certainly deserves to be
indicted, and not allowed to give the truth in evidence.

6. About the Carter Mountain matter.

Some of our good democrats, as it behoveth them,
have strenuously denied the fact of Mr. Jefferson's master-

Than like *un*-philosophic hot-head
To run the risk of being shot dead.

ly retreat from Charlottesville to Carter's Mountain. Now, although we propose to proceed at least to the end of the Canto, stating "false facts" in favour of the subject of our present eulogy, yet we propose to *lie* with somewhat more caution than Mr. Jefferson's advocates have generally done. We therefore will state what some of the wicked federalists have asserted, and leave it to some of our fellow-labourers in the vineyard of democracy, *to lie down* such opposition.

Mr. Smith of South Carolina, in his impudent pamphlet, to which we have referred before (see pages 105 and 110, vol. 1.) has the following allegations against Mr. Jefferson :

" Mr. Jefferson has generally sacrificed the civil rights of his countrymen to his own personal safety. We are told in a public address, by Mr. Charles Simms, of Virginia, who must have been well acquainted with the circumstances, " that Mr. Jefferson, when *governor* of Virginia, *abandoned the trust* with which he was charged, at the moment of an invasion by the enemy, by which, great confusion, *loss and distress, accrued to the state,* in the destruction of public records and vouchers for general expenditures.*

----

* Mr. *Leven Powell, of Virginia, also states, in his public address, " That when* Tarleton, *with a few lighthorse, pursued the assembly to Charlottesville, Mr. Jefferson discovered such a want of firmness, as shewed he was not

Such saving prudence mark'd a sage
A *great man* of a former age,—

"Now, here was a period of public danger, when Mr.
Jefferson's attachment to the civil rights of his countrymen, might have shone very conspicuously, by facing and
averting the danger; here would have been a fine opportunity for him to have displayed his public spirit, in brave-
ly *rallying* round the standard of liberty and civil rights;
but, though in times of safety, he could *rally* round the
standard of his friend, Tom Paine, yet, when real danger
appeared, the *governor of the ancient dominion* dwindled
into the *poor, timid philosopher*; and instead of rallying
his brave countrymen, he fled for safety from a few light-
horsemen, and shamefully abandoned his trust.†

---

fit to fill the first executive office; *for, instead of using his*
talents, in directing the necessary operations of defence,
he quitted his government *by resigning* HIS OFFICE;
this too, at a time which tried men's souls; at a time when
the affairs of America stood in doubtful suspense, and required the exertions of all." *The Governor of Virginia,*
during the invasion *of the state, by a* small *British force,*
instead of defending *the commonwealth at that alarming*
juncture, voluntarily and suddenly surrendered his office,
and at that crisis, his country was required to choose ano-
ther Governor! Is there any security *he would not act*
in like manner again, *in like circumstances?*

† *This charge has been attempted to be got rid of, by*
producing a vote of the assembly of Virginia, after an in-

One Falstaff, famous as our head man,
Thought *honour* nothing in a dead man.

There is likewise one Thomas Turner, Esq. of Virginia,
a gentleman of very respectable character, &c. &c. but
we are somewhat apprehensive that he is a federalist, and
as such, *in our capacity of Eulogist to Mr. Jefferson,* we
shall most assuredly take the liberty to be very severe upon
him, for stating the following most abominable TRUTHS
(for, "the greater the truth, the greater the libel") against
Mr. Jefferson.

" At the time Petersburgh was occupied by the British
troops, under command of Generals Philips and Arnold,
Mr. Jefferson, who was then governor of the state, did
participate in the partial consternation excited by the
situation of the British army, and *did abandon* the seat
of *government,* at a period, and with an awkward pre-
cipitation, indicative of timidity, unwarranted by any

quiry into his conduct, acknowledging his ability and integrity, are altogether silent on his want of firmness, which
had been the cause of his flight.

" It was natural for his friends in the assembly to varnish over this business as well as they could ; and the danger being past, there being no prospect of his being again
exposed in that station, and his flight proceeding not
from any criminality, but from a constitutional weakness
of nerves, it was no difficult matter to get such a vote
from the assembly ; more especially, as the character of
the state was no less implicated in the business than that
of the governor."

B

But being Governor of the State,
(Some carping folks presume to say't,)
He ought t' have stood some little fray,
Smelt powder ere he ran away.

immediate movement of the enemy, and forbidden by a regard to those duties, which belong to the station he held. This fact is well recollected, and can be proved by many of the oldest and most respectable inhabitants of the city of Richmond, and I believe would not be denied by the *candid* supporters of Mr. Jefferson himself.

"The sequel of his conduct, after the assembly returned to Charlottesville, and on the approach of Colonel Tarleton, to that place, stands attested by thousands of witnesses, and can never be forgotten by those of his countrymen, who respect the character of a firm and virtuous public officer, and who abhor that of the dastardly traitor to the trust reposed in him. His retreat, or rather his *flight* from *Monticello*, on the information that Tarleton had penetrated the country, and was advancing to Charlottesville, was effected with such hurried abruptness, as to produce a fall from his horse, and a dislocation of the shoulder. In this situation he proceeded about sixty miles south, to the county of Bedford, whence he forwarded his resignation to the assembly (who had in the mean time removed to Staunton, and) who thereupon elected General Nelson governor. The circumstances are *substantially* and *literally* true ; nay, the abdication of the government must be a matter of record."

Modern philosophers know better
Than their most noble minds to fetter,—
Their new-school principles disparage
With *honour, honesty* and *courage*.

Besides, 'tis said by other some
That charity begins at home,
That each man should take care of one,
Nor fight when there is room to run.

It is moreover my desire
That Turner be esteem'd a liar,
Convict, by Duane's Declaration,
And hung for *theft* and *defamation*.[7]

7 And hung for *theft* and *defamation*.

The *very respectable* editor of the Aurora, as well as
his compeers; Mr. Richie of the Richmond Enquirer,
Mr. Paine and other democratic writers, have shown wonderful adroitness in parrying the thrusts which have been
made at Mr. Jefferson's character. Some have said that
the accusations, provided they were all *true*, amounted to
nothing. Others have undertaken to prove the whole a
parcel of federal lies. But the Aurora-man has attacked
the character of Mr. Turner, in order to invalidate his testimony with so much vigour, that the same Mr. Turner will
never be able to show his head among *honest men*. He has

And I'll make plain as College Thesis,
Our Chief as bold as Hercules is,
By proofs which must confound at once,
Each carping, scurrilous Fed'ral dunce.

A Chief who stands not shilly shally,
But is notorious for—a *Sally* [8]

told a comical, and, *what is wonderful, in part, a true
story,* how one Tom Turner stole a cloak from a member
of congress from Virginia. But the editor of the Evening
Post has spoiled the whole, by the following explanation:
" The truth is, the cloak in question belonged to Mr.
William Hillhouse, member of congress from Connecticut, and it was taken from him by one Mr. Thomas Turner, or as Duane has it, *Tom Turner ;* but *Tom Turner,*
instead of the respectable Virginia planter, who wrote the
letter to Dr. Park, was a man of the same name, who
belonged to the Philosophical Society of Philadelphia, of
which Mr. Jefferson was President; and what is more, he
was like pillory-Nichols, of Boston, and Callender, one of
Mr. Jefferson's confidential CORRESPONDENTS."

8 And is notorious for—a *Sally.*

This line contains, we think, what Edmund Burke
would call " high matter." Indeed, we are far from being
positive, that we are not in this place somewhat *beyond our
own comprehension ;* an error of which, we are the more
apprehensive, as we have observed it to be a common
fault among those writers who advocate democratic poli-

Might Mars defy, in war's dire tug,
Or Satan to an Indian hug.

Therefore ye Feds, if ye should now hard
Things mutter of a nerveless coward,
'Twill prove your characters, ye quizzes,
Black as an Empress's black phiz is.

'Tis true some wicked wags there are,
Who laugh about this dark affair,
But I can tell this shameles faction
They ought t' admire the same transaction;

And did they rightly comprehend
How *means* are sanction'd by the *end*,
They'd change their grumbling tones sar-
To eulogies encomiastic.   [castic

'Tis our right-worshipful belief,
This fine example of our Chief,

tics. We think, therefore, that it will be most judicious
for us to leave it to our commentators to decide, whether,
by the term *Sally*, we mean an attack upon an *enemy*, or
dalliance with a *friend*.

B 2

Of *commerce* join'd to *manufactures*
Makes in his character no fractures:

And we will prove, sans disputation,
Our Chief has wondrous calculation ;
In politics nine times as able
As Mazarine or Machiavel.

For where's a readier resource
For that sweet " social intercourse,"
Which at a grand inauguration
Was promis'd this our happy nation ?

And if, by his example, he goes
To recommend the raising negroes,
The chance is surely in his favour
Of being President forever.

A southern negro is you see, man,
Already three-fifths of a freeman,
And when Virginia gets the staff,
He'll be a freeman and a half.9

9 He'll be a freeman and a half.

The preponderance which Virginia has already obtained in the scale of representation, will enable her to

Great men can never lack supporters,
Who manufacture their own voters;
Besides 'tis plain as yonder steeple,
They will be *fathers* to the people.

And 'tis a decent, clever, comica,
New mode of being economical;
For when a black is rais'd, it follows
It saves a duty of ten dollars.[19]

proceed to increase the privileges of her black population. In this she will be governed by the strict rules of
republican propriety, which always consults the *greatest*
good of the *greatest number*.

10 It saves a duty of ten dollars.

This is a duty, which has been proposed, and probably
will at some future period, be adopted in the southern
states, to prevent the importation of slaves. It is surprising, that, among all the calculations which have distinguished our penny-saving administration, this pleasant
scheme has not been adopted more generally. But a word
to the wise will not be thrown away. Our southern na-
bobs will improve on this hint: sable nabobbesses will
be all the rage; and establishments for the manufacturing
of slaves, will be as common as those for gin or whiskey.

Besides, sir opposition-prater,
That foul reproach to human nature,
The most nefarious guinea trade
May fall by presidential aid.

And he's a wayward blockhead, who says
This making negroes or pappooses
Is not accordant with the plan
Of Tom Paine's precious "Rights of Man."

Therefore, your best and and wisest course
With Antifeds to join your forces,   [is
And all combine to daub and gloss over
Our philanthropical Philosopher.

I know it has been urged by some,
That he who has a wife at home
Flesh of his flesh, bone of his bone,
Might let mulatto girls alone.

But they who say it must be fools
In doctrines of th' illumin'd schools;
Not one can cobble human nature,
Or make a modern Legislator :—

Indeed, they show in this respect
So small a reach of intellect,   [ing
They must have shallow pates, command-
Scarce one inch depth of understanding.

One whose philanthropy's embrace
Incloses all the human race ;
Is forc'd full many schemes to try,
Where more is meant than meets the eye.

All kinds of cattle, 'tis agreed,
Improve whene'er you cross the breed,
With sheep and hogs it is the case,
And eke the jacobinic race.

We therefore think it best to tether
Your blacks and democrats together ;
For in this pleasant way 'tis said
The lustiest patriots may be bred.

And we've no doubt this making brats
Between your blacks and Democrats,
Will serve like varnish or japan
For perfecting the race of man.

Fine scheme ! the more we turn it over,
The more its beauties we discover;
This intercourse of blacks and whites
Will set the wicked world to rights.

Behold the Hartford Mercury-man
Adopts with ardour this new plan,¹¹
Will doubtless aid us in his station,
To bring it into operation.

11 Adopt with ardour this new plan.

In the *Mercury*, a democratic newspaper, was re-pub
lished from the National Intelligencer, a paper, under the
immediate patronage of Mr. Jefferson, a precious paragraph, prettily prefaced as follows:
"THOUGHTS ON THE TRUE PATH TO NATIONAL
GLORY."
"The course of events will likewise inevitably lead to
a mixture of the *whites* and *blacks;* and as the former are
about five times as numerous as the latter, the blacks will
ultimately be merged in the whites. This, indeed, appears to be the great provison made by nature, and, view-
ing the subject in its political aspects, we cannot feel too
much satisfaction at there being an ultimate issue, however remote, independent of the exertions of statesmen,
which, *notwithstanding* its *repugnance to our reason,* as
well as prejudice, will arrive."
No doubt, Mr. Mercury-man!—a most happy expe-
dient truly!—"notwithstanding its repugnance to our

A nd other ministerial prints,
(No doubt from Presidential hints)
Are all alive upon this topic,
So pleasant, and so philanthropic.

The more the thing we look at, true 'tis,
The more we see its myriad beauties,
For this most precious plan discovers
A new and charming field for lovers.

reason" !—And what mortal can sufficiently admire thy wonderful magnanimity, O thou! the GREAT MAN, whom we are humbly attempting to eulogize, in the being one of the first to *put in practice* this philanthropic plan by virtue of which, " the blacks will ultimately be merged in the whites. " !

What say you, O ye fair daughters of Columbia! (we mean the *white ones*) will ye be pleased with a hymeneal lottery, for the purposes aforesaid, in which every fifth lady-adventurer shall draw the delectable prize of a *black* paramour?

But as this notable scheme is of democratic origin, it would be the heighth of impudence for your *old-fashion-ed, un-*philosophical federalists, to interfere in the least. No—the benefits which may result from ths motley mix-ture, and scheme aforesaid, ought to be shared exclu-sively among *genuine* democrats. Those alone will be found worthy to walk in

" THE TRUE PATH TO NATIONAL GLORY."

Each flaxen-headed swain will trill his
Love, song to woollen-pated Phillis!
And pining Corydons will bilk
Their Mistresses of buttermilk !

Each flaunting buckish tippy bobby,
Will take a black wench for his hobby,
And Belles keep fashionable honeys,
Crow-colour'd loves, like Desdemona's.

And none but fools and arrant asses
Will care for " pale.unripen'd" lasses,
Who can succeed to storm the trenches
Of blooming beautiful black wenches ! !

And when in billing kisses sweet
Pasteboard and blubber lips shall meet,
'Twill be allow'd such love surpasses
E'en *nectar* sweeten'd with *molasses !*

Besides our *daughters* and our *wives,*
If happily this project thrives,
Will strengthen Jefferson's resources
By Sambo's social intercourses.

And pray friend Babcock send your wife,
(Now while your theory is rife)
Or bid your daughter sans a fee, go
And practice on it with a negro.

The uglier monster too the better,
But should you hesitate to let her,
'Twill prove the scandalous hypocrisy,
Of your pretensions to democracy.

All hail Columbia's transmutation
To one great grand mulatto nation !
And may success attend each dally,
Of Mr. Jefferson and Sally !

But left this subject so adorable,
To future bards who may be more able ;
In lays supernal and amazing,
To set it absolutely blazing ;

We will pass on and find out whether,
We cannot find another feather,
Or sprig of laurel, which may hap
To fit his Mightiness's cap.

C

Our noble Chieftain is, I wist,
The most renown'd philanthropist,
That ever yet has hatch'd a plan
That went to meliorating man:

Has form'd a scheme, which we delight in,
To stop the horrid trade of fighting ; [13]

12 To stop the horrid trade of fighting!

To prove what a prodigiously benevolent sort of a gentleman we have taken the liberty to eulogize ; and to furnish our readers with a most delightful specimen of close,
accurate, and invincible logic, we will oblige them with
some extracts of a letter from Mr. Jefferson to Sir John
Sinclair, President of the Board of Agriculture at London, dated March 23, 1798, but lately republished in the
democratic papers, by way of applauding the passive
obedience and non-resistance measures of our *creeping*
administration.

" I am fixed with awe (says our Chieftain) at the
mighty conflict, in which two great nations are advancing, and recoil with horror at the ferociousness of man.*

---

* *We cannot but observe, that Mr. Jefferson's being so
terribly terrified at the thoughts of shedding human blood,
even in a " mighly conflict," is a total departure from the
principles of his sect of philosophers.   The illuminati in
general, and Mr. Godwin in particular, have no scruples
of that sort. See Note 53. p. 76. Vol. I.*

Bid England cease from war's alarms,
And Buonapart' lay down his arms !

Will nations never devise a more rational umpire of dif.
ferences than that of force? Are there no means of *coerc-
ing* injustice, more *gratifying* to our nature, than a waste
of the blood of thousands, and the labour of millions of our
fellow-creatures? We see numerous societies of men (the
aboriginals of this country) living together, without the
acknowledgment of either laws or magistracy, yet they
live in peace among themselves, and acts of violence and.
injury are as rare in their societies as in nations which
keep the sword of the law in perpetual activity. Public-
reproach, a refusal of common offices, interdiction of the-
commerce and comforts of society are found as *essential*
as the coarser instrument of force. Nations like these in-
dividuals stand towards each other only in the relations of
natural right. Might they not like them be *peaceably
punished* for violence and wrong ?" &c. &c.

Now let us look at, and of course, as in duty bound,
admire this stream of humanity issuing from the fountain
of philanthropy. What a sublime idea is that of provi-
ding a " rational umpire of differences" between warring
nations who shall " coerce injustice" by " means gratifying to our nature," and teach them to

———feel " the halter draw,
With good opinion of the law."

And because a parcel of American savages, sparsely
scattered over immense wilds, "live without the acknowledgment of either laws or magistracy, in peace among

That is to pacify all nations,
By fine palavering proclamations,
Stating in lieu of cannon's thunder,
'Tis *unpolite* to rob and plunder.

themselves," &c. how very logically follows the *ergo* the
populous, ambitious, and powerful nations of the old world
may.be *ruled* by Mr. Jefferson's notions of " *the relations.*
of right," and warring empires, as well as hostile indivi-
duals be *peaceably punished by* " public reproach, a refusal of common offices," &c. *

Now were we not absolutely and *bona fide* determined
to be Mr. Jefferson's advocate, we should first pick a quarrel with his premises, and then proceed to knock down
his conclusions. We should say that the aboriginals of
this country have their Chiefs, who have the authority of
magistrates; that they are far from always *living at*
peace among themselves, but *murder* is among others, a
common crime, and sometimes a whole tribe is extin-
guished in cold blooded revenge of accidental homicide ;
that their wars are as bloody as those of civilized nations,
and that they generally torture and put their prisoners to
death, with fiend-like malice and ingenuity.

---

* *This mode of subduing the refractory was probably*
invented by Mr. Gallatin, who in his whiskey insurrec-
tion concern, was chairman of a committee of insurgents,
who resolved *to have no intercourse nor dealings with the*
officers of government, to " withdraw from them every as-
sistance, and withhold all the comforts of life," &c.

The only obstacle I see to't,
Is, that some rascals won't agree to't ;
For spite of all our Chief can say,
They will go on and fight away !

But then he shows the good he would do,
Provided, what he would he could do ;
And when a man's a good intention,
He ought said good intent to mention.

And I'd rely with all my heart,
On his persuading Buonapart'
To give us liberty, as much
As France has done the Swiss and Dutch.

All this indeed might be said by Mr. Jefferson's opponents. But *we* would by no means be guilty of such an
ill-advised attack on such fine *practical* philosophy, and
recommend to this great philanthropist, and his sagacious adherents to rely altogether on the *perfectibility* of human nature, and the probability of nations submitting to
be *peaceably* punished without any force, in some way
gratifying to our nature. And therefore we would have
them set about destroying the remains of our navy, army,
forts, arsenals, &c. &c. so that it may not be possible for
us to engage in any of those " mighty conflicts," which
cause Mr. Jefferson such excess of trepidation.

C 2

Then don't let fed'ralists provoke him,
And Mr. Jefferson will stroke him,
Till he will condescend, I trow,
Our commonwealth to take in tow.

No doubt our bright affairs with Spain,
Are in their present happy train,
In consequence of our sweet temper,
And President who's *idem semper.*

But should we chance to think that our
Security consists in pow'r,
Negociate with our arms in hand,
The Lord knows only where we'll land.

Most of our democrats know fully,
That *lying down* disarms a bully ;
That *nothing* ever is a stranger
To *every thing* that looks like danger.

And doubtless French and Algerines,
Will be persuaded by such means,
'Tis best to let alone our commerce,
Nor take our hard-earn'd money from us.

Therefore I say, and will maintain,
The man must be a rogue in grain,
Who won't acknowledge our good Presi-
    dent,
The greatest man on this earth resident.

Though Gossip Fame has been a talker,
Of some attempts at Mrs. Walker ; 13

13 Of some attempts at Mrs. Walker.

Here we shall be obliged, once more, to be severe on the before-mentioned Thomas Turner, Esq. for having the temerity to tattle slander against the man, whom good democrats delight to honour.

" The father of Colonel John Walker (says this man, who thinks he can "tell truth and shame the devil") was the guardian of Mr. Jefferson, and advanced a part of those funds, which were applied to the education of the latter; an education affording those talents, which have been so strangely perverted, which have been insidiously employed in the conception of schemes, foul, ungrateful,, horrible. At a very early period of their lives, Colonel Walker and Mr. Jefferson contracted an attachment which grew up with their years and ripened into the closest intimacy.—Their professions were mutual ; their confidence unbounded. While things were in this situation, Mr. Jefferson was meditating the unnatural purpose of seducing the wife of his best friend, and to this end (taking advan-

Yet this is silly, slanderous stuff,
Or if 'twere true 'tis *right enough.*

tage of the confidence of Colonel Walker, and availing himself of the timidity of the lady, whose affection for her husband prevented the disclosure of a transaction, which might lead to an exposure of his life) devoted himself for ten. years, repeatedly and assiduously making attempts, which were as repeatedly, and with horror repelled. For *ten years* was this purpose pursued, and at last abandoned (*as he himself acknowledges*) from the inflexible virtue of the lady, and followed (as he also acknowledges) by the deepest and most heart-wounding remorse."*

All this I HAVE SEEN: NOT in newspapers; not in extracts; not in copies of letters.—I HAVE SEEN IT in the ORIGINAL CORRESPONDENCE BETWEEN MESSRS. WALKER AND JEFFERSON, every letter of which bears the signature of the writer, or has been since acknowledged by him, under his own hand. In this correspondence Mr. Jefferson repeatedly and fervently confesses that the guilt is all his own; the innocence all Mrs. Walker's; and that he shall never cease to revere, and attest the purity of her character, and deprecate his unpardonable and unsuccessful attempt to destroy her. His contrition, his misery, are asserted in the warmest terms, and his acquittal of Mrs. Walker pronounced in the strongest language of

---

* *The reader will please to observe, that this remorse of Mr. Jefferson, so unworthy a philosophist, took place before his.*illumination. C. C.

Your pure professors of perfection,
In morals can have no defection ;

his pen. Among other concessions he owns, that in order to cover the real cause of the separation between Colonel Walker and himself, he did FABRICATE a NOTE respecting an unsettled account which he said had produced the schism, and which he expressly acknowledges HAD NO FOUNDATION IN TRUTH. Let it not be forgotten that the attempts against the honour of Mrs. Walker were carried on DURING THE LIFE TIME OF MRS. JEFFERSON, than whom a better woman and better wife never existed."

And must the head of a great nation, the idol of a *free* people, and the patron of Tom Paine, be lacerated and scarified in this manner? Surely not with impunity, for lo, Tom Paine hath taken up the gauntlet in his defence! and now it behoveth all who would not choose to be buried alive in the filth of obloquy, to sneak out of the scrape of opposition to Mr. Jefferson, with all possible celerity. The letter of Mr. Turner, says the author of the Age of Reason, and the enemy of WASHINTON, and the friend of Mr. Jefferson, is a *" putrid production,"* but " having nothing else to do" he has "thrown away an hour or two," in " examining its component parts." Mr. Turner and Mr. Hurlburt, (the latter is the gentleman, who distinguished himself by a famous speech in the Legislature of Massachusetts, in the laudable attack made by the minority of that body on the liberty of the press) he politely stiles " *two skunks who stink in concert.*" This is succeeded by other *arguments* at least as convincing, and as delicately expressed, but somewhat too " *lengthy*" for insertion.

Like *upright* people, so particular,
They stand up *more* than perpendicular.

And I've no doubt but what this scandal,
Is nothing but a federal handle,
To blast our Emp'ror's fame, who's not
Than Scipio or Joseph spotless.   [less

But protest enter'd first, I may
Just mention what some people say,
Who ought to suffer bastinading,
For crime of President-degrading.

Some say 'twas vile ingratitude,
In Mr. Jefferson, so rude,
To attack his benefactor's wife,
The pride, the solace of his life ;—

The virtuous woman to annoy,
By siege as long as that of Troy,
And bring bad principles to aid [14]
His systematical blockade.

14 And bring bad principles to aid.

We have heard it reported by some vilifier of Mr. Jef-

But I'll maintain he is consistent,
His conduct has n't a single twist in't ;
If having *twenty Gods,* he drives
To have at least as many wives.

Among your new-school rights and duties,
There's no monopoly of beauties, [15]
And he's a churl, who will not lend
His pretty wife t' oblige a friend.

No man, who is not old and frigid,
Or most unconscionably rigid,
Will e'er " oppugnate" this morality
Of such a pretty genteel quality:

And were all true which is related
About a note once fabricated,

-ferson, that he endeavoured to induce Mrs. Walker to
compliance with his wishes, by putting in her way certain *sentimental* treatises, said to be proper on such occasions.

15 There's no monopoly of beauties.

For some further illustration of this delectable doctrine,
we would refer our reader to p. 57, Note 45. Vol. I.

By which his highness did intend
To ruin one he call'd his friend;

'Twas right to set himself a brewing
This cross-grain'd lady's husband's ruin,
Who, had he been polite, had chuckled
At chance to be a great man's cuckold.

From such examples men may chance
To learn your true French complaisance,
And married prudes to put no cross over
The wishes of a great philosopher.

Though he imported Thomas Paine,
(For Chronicleers have lied in vain,)[16]

16 (For Chronicleers have lied in vain.)

The Boston Chronicle, and we believe many other democratic papers, declared that the report of Mr. Jefferson's having invited Paine to return to this country, was a falsehood of federal fabrication, invented on purpose to slander Mr. Jefferson. But, when Paine published the letter, with that accommodating versatility, which is no doubt absolutely necessary for the support of their party, they applauded the President for that very measure. The letter itself is couched in terms highly respectful, and

T' oppose with acrimonious vanity,
Law, order, morals, and christianity.

'Twas right, for aught I can discover,
To send and fetch the fellow over,
For Freedom, by his aid may chance
With us to flourish as in France.[16]

is highly honorary to both parties in the correspondence. The following are extracts:

" DEAR SIR,

" Your letters of Oct. 1st, 4th, 6th, 16th, came duly to hand, and the papers which they covered were, according to your permission, published in the newspapers, and under your own name. These papers contain precisely our principles, and I hope they will be generally recognised here.

" You expressed a wish to get a passage to this country in a public vessel. Mr. Dawson is charged with orders to the captain of the Maryland to receive and accommodate you back, if you can be ready to depart at such a short warning.

" That you may long live to continue your *useful* labours, and to reap the reward in the thankfulness of nations, is my sincere prayer. Accept assurances of my high esteem and affectionate attachment."

16 With us to flourish as in France.

Paine has given us a specimen, in one of his letters to the citizens of the United States, of the success of his

The man who has such service done,
By neat abuse of Washington,[17]

labours in the cause of liberty in that genuine republican country. Robespierre seized him, together with many other *eminent patriots*, and imprisoned him eleven months, proposed to requite his revolutionary services with the guillotine. The downfal of the tyrant, however, prevented this termination to Paine's political labour, and the arch Infidel has come, *not* to infect this country with the poison of his seditious and blasphemous publication, but, as Mr Jefferson says, to " continue his useful labours among us."

But it somehow unfortunately happens, that Tom Paine's merits are not fully appreciated by certain of Mr. Jefferson's admirers. In a newspaper entitled the Freeman's Journal, established under the auspices of Governor M'Kean & Co. at Philadelphia, we find Mr. Tom Paine's quondam friends attacking him in a most merciless manner. We will give a short paragraph as a specimen of the unmerited abuse which is lavished on this almost a martyr, in the cause of licentiousness and infidelity.

" Had this polluted monster remained in France, he would have conferred a particular favour on this country. Infamous and execrated, he might have "gone to his' own place," unheeded and unregarded, like any other outcast from society. But, as if the measure of his iniquity was not yet full, this foe to God and man has come hither to plague us."

Deserves the highest approbation
From our great *tip-end* of the nation.

But let Mr. Tom Paine never seem to mind a little *quid* abuse, for he has received "*assurances of*" Mr. Jefferson's " high esteem and affectionate attachment."

17 By neat abuse of Washington.

A specimen or two of delicate invective, taken from Paine's letter to George Washington, President of the United States, dated Paris, July 30th, 1796, and printed by Benjamin Franklin Bache, the worthy predecessor of William Duane, the present editor of the Aurora, will doubtless very much oblige our good democratic readers and show what a well qualified champion Mr. Jefferson has enlisted in his defence.

" I declare myself opposed to almost the whole of your administration; for I know it to be deceitful, if not even perfidious."

" Injustice was acted under pretence of faith ; and the Chief of the army became the patron of the fraud."

· " Meanness and ingratitude have nothing equivocal in their character. There is not a trait in them that renders them doubtful. They are so original vices, that they are generated in the dung of other vices, and crawl into existence with the filth upon their back. The fugitives have found protection in you, and the levee room is the place of their rendezvous."

Moreover 'tis a proper season
To burnish up the " Age of Reason,"
Lest, peradventure, too much piety
Sap the foundations of society.

And we moreover understand, he
Supports the state—by drinking brandy,
And if he lives, will free the nation
From debt,.without direct taxation.

But though our Chief to all intents is
A paragon of excellencies,
The wicked Feds are always prating
Matter the most calumniating.

For I've heard many a crabbed Fed,
While things like these he muttering said,

" The character which Mr. Washington has attempted
to act in the world, is a sort of non-describable, camelion
coloured thing, called *prudence*."

" As to you, Sir, treacherous in private friendship, and
a hypocrite in public life, the world will be puzzled to decide whether you are an apostate, or an impostor; whether you have abandoned good principles, or whether
you ever had any," &c. &c.

T' oppose with acrimonious vanity,
Law, order, morals, and christianity.

'Twas right, for aught I can discover,
To send and fetch the fellow over,
For Freedom, by his aid may chance
With us to flourish as in France.[16]

is highly honorary to both parties in the correspondence. The following are extracts:

"DEAR SIR,

"Your letters of Oct. 1st, 4th, 6th, 16th, came duly to hand, and the papers which they covered were, according to your permission, published in the newspapers, and under your own name. These papers contain precisely our principles, and I hope they will be generally recognised here.

"You expressed a wish to get a passage to this country in a public vessel. Mr. Dawson is charged with orders to the captain of the Maryland to receive and accommodate you back, if you can be ready to depart at such a short warning.

"That you may long live to continue your *useful* labours, and to reap the reward in the thankfulness of nations, is my sincere prayer. Accept assurances of my high esteem and affectionate attachment."

16 With us to flourish as in France.

Paine has given us a specimen, in one of his letters to the citizens of the United States, of the success of his

The man who has such service done,
By neat abuse of Washington,[17]

labours in the cause of liberty in that genuine republican country. Robespierre seized him, together with many other *eminent patriots,* and imprisoned him eleven months, proposed to requite his revolutionary services with the guillotine. The downfal of the tyrant, however, prevented this termination to Paine's political labour, and the arch Infidel has come, *not* to infect this country with the poison of his seditious and blasphemous publication, but, as Mr Jefferson says, to " continue his useful labours among us."

But it somehow unfortunately happens, that Tom Paine's merits are not fully appreciated by certain of Mr. Jefferson's admirers. In a newspaper entitled the Freeman's Journal, established under the auspices of Governor M'Kean & Co. at Philadelphia, we find Mr. Tom Paine's quondam friends attacking him in a most merciless manner. We will give a short paragraph as a specimen of the unmerited abuse which is lavished on this almost a martyr, in the cause of licentiousness and infidelity.

" Had this polluted monster remained in France, he would have conferred a particular favour on this country. Infamous and execrated, he might have " gone to his own place," unheeded and unregarded, like any other outcast from society. But, as if the measure of his iniquity was not yet full, this foe to God and man has come hither to plague us."

With great pretence to Mathematics,
I'd ask, is his report on Staticks,

quence to their prosperity. And shall we refuse to the un-
happy fugitives from distress that hospitality, which the
savages of the wilderness extended to our fathers arriving
in this land? Shall oppressed humanity find no assylum
on this globe? Might not the general character and ca-
pabilities of a citizen be safely communicated to *every
one* manifesting a *bona fide* purpose of embarking his life
and fortune permanently with us?"

In the Notes on Virginia we also learn, " That the political economists of Europe have established it as a principle, that every state should manufacture for itself: and the
principle like many others we transfer to America, without calculating the different circumstances, which should
often produce a different result. In Europe, the lands
are either cultivated, or locked up against the cultivation.
Manufacture must, therefore, be resorted to of necessity,
not of choice, to support the surplus of their people. But
we have an immensity of land, courting the industry of
the husbandman. Is it best, then, that *all our citizens*
should be employed in its improvement, or, that one half
should be called off from that, to exercise manufacture
and handicrafts for the other? Those who labour in the
earth are the chosen people of God, *if ever he had a chosen people*; whose breasts he has made the peculiar de-
posit for substantial and genuine virtue.—It is the *focus*
in which he keeps alive that sacred fire, which otherwise
might escape from the earth. Corruption of morals in the
mass of cultivators is a phenomenon of which no age nor

And Standard Measures worth a fig ?[19]
No ; 'twould disgrace the learned pig.

nation has furnished an example. It is the mark set on
those who, not looking up to heaven, to their own soil and
to industry, as does the husbandman, for their subsistence, depend for it on the casualties and caprice of cus-
tomers.   Dependence begets subservience and venality ;
suffocates the germ of virtue, and prepares fit tools for the
designs of ambition.   This, the natural progress and consequence of the arts has sometimes perhaps been retard-
ed by accidental circumstances: but generally speaking,
the proportion which the aggregate of the other classes of
the citizens bears, in any state, to that of its husbandmen,
is the proportion of its unsound to its healthy parts, and
is a good enough barometer, whereby to measure its degree of corruption.   While we have land to labour let us
never wish to see our citizens occupied at a work-bench
or twirling a distaff.   Carpenters and smiths are wanting
in husbandry: but for the general operation of manufacture, let our workshops remain in Europe.   It is better to
carry provisions and materials to workmen there, than
bring them to the provisions and materials, and with them
their manners and principles.   The loss, by the transpor-
tation of commodities across the atlantic will be made up
in happiness and permanence of government.   The mobs
of great cities add just so much to the support of pure government, as sores do to the strength of the human body."
   The above was written in 1782. In the year 1793, Mr.
Jefferson, then Secretary of State, having occasion to fall
out with Great Britain, in a report relative to com-

Some *borrowed* things are well enough,[20]
But all his *own* is stupid stuff,

mercial restrictions of other nations, and the measures
which the United States ought to pursue to counteract
them, recommends the imposition of heavy duties, or
excluding such foreign manufactures as we take in greatest quantities, for " Such duties (he observes) having the
effect of, indirect encouragement to domestic manufactures of the same kind may, *induce the manufacturer to
come himself* into these States ; and here it would be in
the power of the State governments to cooperate essen-
tially, by opening the resources of encouragement which
are under their controul, extending them liberally to artists in those particular branches of manufactures for
which their soil, climate, population, and other circumstances have matured them, and fostering the precious
efforts and progress of household manufacture, by some
patronage suited to the nature of its objects, guided by
the local information they possess, and guarded against
abuse by their presence and attention. The oppressions
on our agriculture in foreign parts would thus be made the
occasion of relieving it from a dependence on the coun-
cils and conduct of others, and *promoting arts, manufactures* and *population* at home."

Mr. Jefferson's Message contained the first proposition
for an attack on the judiciary, and he is well known to
have gone hand in hand with his estimable party, in the
courageous and successful inroad made on the aristocratic
constitution of the United States, by putting down the

And goes with fifty proofs beside ·
To prove his *head* and *heart* allied.[21]

federal judges by the dozen. That in this respect he has made great improvements in the theory of liberty, since writing his Notes on Virginia, will abundantly appear from the following quotation from that work, so highly celebrated by the admirers of genuine freedom.

Speaking of the government of Virginia, he remarks, that " All the powers of government, legislative, executive and judiciary, result to the legislative body. The concentrating these in the same hands is precisely the definition of *despotic government*. It will be no alleviation that these powers will be exercised by a plurality of hands, and not by a single one. One hundred and twenty-three despots would surely be as oppressive as one. Let those who doubt it turn their eyes to the republic of Venice. As little will it avail us that they are chosen by ourselves. An *elective despotism* was not the government we fought for ; but one which should not only be founded on free principles, but in which the powers of government should be so divided and balanced among several bodies of magistracy, as that no one should transcend their legal limits without being effectually checked and restrained by the others. For this reason, that convention which passed the ordinance of government, laid its foundation on this basis, that the legislative, executive and judiciary departments should be separate and distinct, so that no person should exercise the powers of more than one of them at the same time. But no barrier was provided between these several powers. The judiciary and executive · members were

Who's vile. enough to be defender
Of his base paper money tender,

left dependent on the legislative for their subsistence in office, and some of them for their continuance in it. If therefore, the legislature assumes executive and judiciary powers; no opposition is likely to be made, nor if made, can be effectual ; because in that case they may put their proceedings into the form of an act of assembly, which will render them obligatory on the other branches. They have accordingly, in many instances, decided rights which should have been left to judiciary controversy ; and the direction of the executive, during the whole time of their session, is becoming habitual and familiar." See Notes on Virginia, Query xii.

One more specimen of Mr. Jefferson's openness to conviction, and the facility with which he relinquishes an error of opinion the moment he discovers it, we shall furnish from his philosophical disquisition on the colour and other properties of negroes. Our philosopher, after stating certain modes by which the evil of slavery in Virginia might be annihilated, such as that the black slaves "should continue with their parents to a certain age, then be brought up, at the public expense, to tillage, arts or sciences, according to their geniusses, till the females should be eighteen, and the males twenty-one years of age, when they should be *colonized* to such place, as the circumstances of the time should render most proper sending vessels at the same time to the other parts of the world for an equal number of white inhabitants," proceeds with the following profound observation : "It will pro-

In which he would defraud, forsooth,
The friend and patron of his youth.

bably be asked, why not retain and incorporate the blacks
in this state ? I answer, deep-rooted prejudices entertain-
ed by the whites, ten thousand recollections by the blacks
of the injuries they have sustained, new provocations, *the
real distinction which nature has made,* and many other
circumstances, will divide us into parties, and produce
convulsions, which will never end but in the extermina-
tion of the *one or the other race.* To these objections,
which are political, may be added others, which are *physical and moral.* The first difference which strikes us, is
that of colour ; whether the black of the negro resides in
the reticular membrane, between the skin and the scarf-
skin, or in the skin itself; whether it proceeds from the
colour of the blood, or the colour of the bile, or from
that of some other secretion, *the difference is fixed in nature,* and is as *real* as if its seat and cause were better
known to us. And is this difference of no importance ?
Is it not the foundation of a greater or less share of beauty
in the two races? Are not the fine mixture of red and
white, the expressions of every passion, by the greater or
less suffusion of colour in the one, preferable to the eternal
monotony, which reigns in the countenances of the other
race? Add to these, flowing hair, a more elegant symmetry
of form, their own judgment in favour of the whites, declared by their preference of them, as uniformly as is the
preference of the ourang-outang for the black women over
those of his own species. Besides those of colour, figure,
and hair, there are other physical distinctions proving a

Ingratitude, of crimes the worst,
In none but serpent-bosoms nurst,

different race ; ~~they~~ have less hair on the face and body ; they secrete less by the kidnies, and more by the glands of the skin, which gives them a very strong and disagreeable odour."

" They are in reason much inferior to the whites. It is not against experience to suppose, that different *species* of the same *genus,* or varieties of the same species may possess different qualifications. Will not a lover of natural history, then, one who views the gradations in all the races of animals, with the eye of philosophy, *excuse an effort to keep those in the department of man as distinct as nature has formed them.*"

He afterwards observes, " that the improvement of the blacks in body and mind, in the first instance of their mixture with the whites, is observed by every one, and *proves that their inferiority* is not the effect merely of their condition in life. Among the Romans, their slaves were often their rarest artists ; they excelled too in science, insomuch as to be employed as tutors to their masters' children. Epictetus, Terence and Phoedrus, were slaves ; but they were of the race of whites. *It is not their condition, then, but* NATURE, which has produced the distinction."

Mr. Jefferson doubtless wrote these observations previous to his having obtained an intimate acquaintance with the good qualities of the blacks. But some subsequent investigations, could not but lead a man of his penetration, to reject any pre-conceived opinion, unfavorable to this

It seems but qualifies a man
To head the democratick clan.

" *race of animals.*"   And instead of keeping those in the
department of man as distinct as possible, he now not only
maintains, that the " *true path to national glory,*" leads
to a mixture of the *whites* and *blacks,* (See note 11, p. 22,
Vol. II.) but has condescended to add *example* to pre·
cept, to teach us by his own experiments the soundness
of his philosophy.

It is probable that the new light, which he obtained
by the only true mode of philosophising, led him to the
candid confessions contained in a congratulatory letter to
his worthy and learned brother, Benjamin Banneker, *said
to be,* the author of an almanack, &c. In this last production, he declared in the teeth of his former theory, that
" he rejoiced to find that *Nature* had given to his *black
brethren* talents equal to those of other colours, and that
the *appearance* of a want of them, was owing *merely* to
the *degraded condition* of their existence, both in Africa
and America."

There is a philosopher of pliability for you! none of
your rigid personages who will remain obstinate in error
against the light of reason, and his own and other men's
experiments.   This whirling to the left about, in consequence of the wonderful phenomenon of a Negro Almanack, (probably enough made by a white man) was as masterly a manœuvre, in a political, as the retreat to Carter's
mountain, in a military point of view.

Was it not scandalous hypocrisy,
To please the looking-on mobocracy,

19 And standard measures worth a fig?

Mr. Jefferson's report on weights and measures has been highly celebrated by his party, but the mischief making Federalists have made many unmerciful strictures on its defects. To show with what kind of logick Mr. Jefferson, has been assailed we shall again have recourse to the pamphlet of Mr. Smith, in which Mr. Jefferson and his pretensions are so roughly handled.

Mr. Jefferson was required "to report to the House a proper plan for establishing uniformity in the currency of weights and measures of the United States."

"The object of a plain, sensible man, more anxious to render solid *services* to the country, than to acquire reputation by a *pedantick* display of science, would naturally have been, to ascertain the existing currency, weights and measures in the United States, and to establish such a *standard*, as would be most conformable to the *general* use, and attended with the least innovation and distress.

"In respect to uniformity in *measures*, nothing more would have been requisite than to have proposed that some determined standard should be made and lodged in some public depository, to which access might be had, when necessary.

"Instead of this, Mr. Jefferson proposes a system, which professes *extreme minuteness, precision and accuracy,* and yet, when examined, is found to *leave every thing to*
E 2

For him to sob, and sigh and groan
O'er the green grave of ·Washington.²²

the skill and accuracy of a Watchmaker ;* a system, de-
pending on *criteria,* which he considered as *important,*
and yet, which are not *defined* in such manner as to
admit of an application of them.

" He begins the report with observing, "that there
exists not in nature a single subject, or species of subject accessible to man, which permits one constant
and uniform dimension." The causes of this variation
of dimension are stated to be *expansion* and *contraction,*
occasioned by change of *temperature.* *Iron* is stated to
be the *least expansible* of *metals,* and the degree of expansion of a pendulum of 58. 7, inches is said to be
from 200 to 300 parts of an inch.

Mr. Jefferson, however, says, "that the globe of the
earth might be considered as *invariable in all its dimensions,* and that its *circumference* would furnish an *invariable measure.*" But if a small portion of the least expansible metal, *iron,* is so affected by *temperature,* how
can it be true, that the globe would furnish an *invariable
measure?* Is not the whole earth, composed as it is of
various elements, all *more* expansible than iron, liable to
be affected by changes of temperature? Are not differ-

" * *Report,* p. 3. " *In order to avoid the* uncertainties
*which respect the centre of oscillation, it has been proposed
by Mr.* Leslie, *an ingenious artist of Philadelphia, to
substitute for the* pendulum, *an uniform cylindrical rod,
without a bob.*"

When this same gentleman had paid
One who set up the lying trade,

ent sides of the earth presented to the sun, at different seasons of the year? Is not the whole globe nearer to the sun in some parts of its orbit, than at others? Is it not, of course, more susceptible of *heat,* and more affected by *attraction,* both of which operate to affect the dimensions of our globe? Is it likely that earth, water, and other elements, are so equally distributed through our globe, as that the degrees of expansion and contraction, occasioned by changes of seasons, exactly counterbalance each other?—Was it not known to Mr. Jefferson, that no two of the great circles of our globe are of equal circumference, and that this rendered his position, at *least doubtful?*

" Mr. Jefferson says, " that no one circle of the globe is accessible to admeasurement in all its parts, and that the trials to measure portions have been of such various result, as to shew that there is no dependence on that operation for certainty. If this be true, what were the *data* upon which it was asserted, that the whole *circumference* would furnish *an invariable measure?* The French philosophers now say the contrary, and they have lately *actually* taken a *section* of the earth for their standard. Who is to decide between these doctors, or are they all aiming to *puzzle* plain people, by an *affectation* of accuracy, which is unattainable?

" Mr. Jefferson's *standard* is " a uniform cylindrical rod of iron, of such length, as in latitude 45 degrees, in the *level of the ocean,* and in a *cellar* or other place, the *temperature* of which does not vary throughout the year, shall

A scoundrel from a foreign nation
To stab that hero's reputation ?[23]

perform its vibrations, in small and equal arcs, in one second of mean time."

"The degree of 45 degrees is assumed, because it was
proposed by France, and because it was the northern
boundary of the United States. He says, "let the
completion of the 45 degrees then give the standard for
our union, with the hope, he *facetiously* adds, that it
may become a *line of union*, with the rest of the world;"
a pleasant conceit! it was kind in this profound philosopher to emerge from the depth of his experimental cellar, to enliven this scientific and *abstruse* subject with a
pun.

"But our philosopher's hope of a *line of union* with the
rest of the world is already defeated; the French, have,
since his report, taken a section of a meridional line for
their standard*. Their pendulum for 45 degrees is to

---

* *Notwithstanding this friendly hope, the French have
treated our philosopher very cavalierly, by altogether dis-
regarding, in their late system, his learned labors.
Though he was so ready to adopt whatever they proposed,
they have not even condescended to take the least notice of
his report. Even Fauchet, in his letter to the secretary
of state, communicating the French standard of weights
and measures, seems not to have even heard of the secretary's report; for he says, " France was the first to place
those researches among the cares of government. America, if I mistake not, has since followed the example, for*

What think you of his double shuffle,
When he and Genet had a scuffle,[24]

vibrate 100,000 seconds, while Mr. Jefferson's is vibrating 86,400.

" The French have outdone even Mr. Jefferson in innovation; thus illusory has the expectation proved, that the hobby-horse of one philosopher will be respected by another.

" But why this *attempt* at absolute accuracy? He admits that the pendulum of 45 degrees differs from the pendulum of 31 degrees, only 1-679 part of its whole length, and that this difference is so minute that it might be *neglected, as insensible for the common purposes of life.* There was some reason for the attempt beyond a display of learning, or there was not; if *perfect exactness* was desirable, why where the following *causes* of *uncertainty* and *error* unnoticed?

" 1st. The experiment, he says, must be made in the *level of the ocean,* to prevent that *increment to the radius of the earth and consequent diminution of the length of the pendulum,* which a higher situation would produce: what is the *level of the ocean?* the tide rises in 45 degrees about fifteen feet, and there are levels of the ocean at *high-water, low-water,* and at *all points* between

———————————————————————

I think I have heard that the present government were engaging in the same changes, and even waited the result of the operation made in France on this subject, for the purpose of commencing their return."

Did it become one in his station
To show so much prevarication ?

these extremes. *Perfect exactness* required that the ex-
pression, *level of the ocean,* should have been defined :
this *omission* has since been rectified in a bill which
passed the House of Representatives last session.*

" 2d. The experiment, says the report, must be made
in a cellar or other p'ace, the temperature of which does
not vary throughout the year. This is *important,* or it is
not : if important, why not *define* the *temperature,* that
it might be ascertained by a thermometer. There are
few or no natural caves or cellars, in which the temperature does not vary : variations are frequently noticed in
the deepest caves and mines : various causes may affect
the temperature : Mr. Jefferson admits this, in his Notes,
p. 21, wheie he allows that " *chymical agents* may produce in subterraneous cavities, a *factitious heat* ;" and
these may more or less, affect the temperature in most
caves or ecllars.

" The *pendulum* is, however, admitted by Mr. Jefferson, to be liable to *uncertainties,* for which he offers no

---

* *That bill directs, that " the experiments shall be
made in the latitude of Philadelphia, at any place between
the rivers Delaware and Schuylkill, at a known height
above the level of common high water in the Delaware,
and in a known temperature of the atmosphere, according
to Farenheit's thermometer.*

Will any democrat declare
That was a very pious prayer,

remedies: how does it appear that these uncertainties are not more important than the causes of error, to which his attention has been directed ?

" 3d. Machinery (says the report, page 8,) and a power are necessary, which may exert a small but con_ stant effort to renew the waste of motion, but so that they shall *neither retard nor accelerate* the vibrations."

" But it adds, in the next page, " to estimate and *obviate this difficulty* is the *artist's province.*" What is this, but to say, that the *standard* of the United States shall be the pendulum of some clock, made by Mr. Leslie, or some other artist, thus *discarding* at once *all reliance* upon the *principles* before advanced. The *difficulty* of ascertaining the centre of oscillation, (which he admits to be impossible, unless in a rod, of which the diameter is " *infinitely small,*") he thinks however *can be obviat-ed* by Mr. Leslie, the watchmaker.

" Mr. Jefferson then proceeds to apply his standard,

" 1st. To *measures of capacity.* These he proposes should be *four-sided,* with rectangular sides and bottom, for which he gives the following reasons : " *cylindrical* measures have the advantage of *superior strength ;* but square ones have the *greater advantage* of *enabling* every one, who has a rule in his pocket, to *verify their contents,* by measuring them." Did it not occur to this profound mathematician, that a man with a *rule* in his pocket, could *as easily* measure the *diameter* and *depth* of a cy-

Which he for Adams, whom he hated,
So solemnly ejaculated ?[25]

lindrical half bushel as the sides and depth of a square box?

" 2d. To *weights*. The standard of weights is proposed to be a definite portion of *rain water*, weighed always in the *same temperature*. " It will be necessary, says he, to refer these weights to a determinate mass of substance, the specifick gravity of which is *invariable*; *rain water* is *such* a substance, and may be referred to every where, and through all time." But the temperature is *not defined;* rain water is *varied* by several causes; dust, insects, &c. will create a difference in its weight. The French, in their late plan, have outdone Mr. Jefferson; their standard is *distilled* water, ascertained by a *defined* temperature."

Such is the cruel manner in which the federal rogues cut up a *genuine* philosopher.

20 Some *borrowed* things are well enough.

A part of Mr. Jefferson's report on weights and measures, was founded on ideas taken from a volume of the society of Arts and Agriculture, published in Europe. The fluxional calculations are the work of a Professor in Columbia College. *See the Minerva, a newspaper printed in New-York, of July,* 1796.

Has he paid nothing to maintain
The press of demagogue Duane,

21 To prove his *head* and *heart* allied,

There is a great affinity between that obliquity of intellect, which leads a man to *think* incorrectly, and that
depravity of heart, which tends to immoral conduct. A
wrong-headed enthusiast, who is addicted to an incorrect
and whimsical mode of reasoning and thinking, may easily allay the qualms of conscience by the opiate of sophism,
and even become what Godwin calls an "*honest assas-
sin.*" Perhaps there have been but few crimes of magni-
tude committed, in which the perpetrators have not been
able to persuade themselves, that they were justifiable, if
not commendable. Religious, political and philosophical enthusiasm have, each in their turn, impelled mankind to deeds of horror, from which the most abandoned
would revolt with abhorrence, if they did not believe
that they were actuated by motives which are praise-
worthy.

The dexterity with which our knight-errants in sedition
reconcile their conduct to the dictates of their reason, is
well exemplified by Butler, in the character of Hudibras,
who thus justifies the breaking of his oath :

"He that imposes an oath makes it,
Not he that for convenience takes it ;
Then how can any man be said
To break an oath he never made."

But these being grave old-school reflections, it would
F

Teeming with foulest defamation
Of Washington's administration.[26]

be very improper to indulge them in a canto, set apart like
this, for celebrating an illuminatus.

22 O'er the green grave of Washington.

It is well known that Mr. Jefferson made a very pretty
and suitable parade of grief at the tomb of General Washington.   And as remarked by a poet in the Utica Patriot,

"A *genuine* tear from a *genuine* chief
Is a *genuine* proof of a *genuine* grief!"

The federal editor of the New-York Evening Post,
in his *aristocratical way* thus remarks upon this subject :
"Will the reader once accompany us to the saddened
groves of Mount-Vernon.   Behold this same Thomas Jefferson at the tomb of Washington! See him approach
the hallowed spot, surrounded by spectators '—he kneels
before the sacred dust !—he weeps outright at the irre-
parable loss of this greatest, best, and most beloved of
men !—sobs choak his utterance! he clasps his hands in
token of pious resignation to the will of heaven, and re-
tires in silence amidst the blessings of those whose sym-
pathy he had beguiled by "presenting his profession of
sorrow."

23 To stab that hero's reputation?

Though the circumstance of Mr. Jefferson's having
paid Callender for his *services* in abuse of the *Federal*

Pray plaster over, if you can, sir,
The foolish and sophistic answer

Constitution, Washington, Adams, and many others of
our revolutionary patriots, is proved by letters written with
his own hand, yet democrats, with that laudable pertina-
city, which is the soul of their party, would never believe
a word about the matter.

" Convince some men against their will,
They're of the same opinion still."

The intelligent and indefatigable editor of the Boston
Repertory, makes the following plaint on the occasion :

" How often have we been stigmatised as infamous
slanderers, for asserting that Mr. Jefferson patronised Callender in his virulent abuse of the *Federal Constitution,*
Washington and Adams. It was a federal lie, and no democrat would yield credit to a circumstance, which, if
true, would exhibit Mr. Jefferson in the blackest colours
of political hypocrisy, and allied to that demon of slander, for the purpose of *lying* down his betters We now
offer irresistible proof—Mr. Jefferson's letters to Callender, in his own hand writing. ONE DEMOCRAT, and
one only, has called to satisfy himself !"

Now this is as it should be. Stick to your party, genuine republicans ! right or wrong.

Our good democrats, with the greatest propriety, as it
adds to their popularity, are always fond of uniting the
names of Washington and Jefferson.   That Mr. Jefferson was friendly to General Washington, and his administration, will appear from the following *elegant extracts.*

Which his sublimity did dish up
About th'appointment of old Bishop.

taken from the " Prospect before Us," at that time patronised and its specimen sheets inspected by *Mr Jefferson*:

Speaking of General V.ashington, Mr. Jefferson's editor says, " He could not have committed a more pure
and *net violation of his oath* to preserve the constitution,
and of his official trust ; or a grosser personal insult on
the representatives."

" By his own account, Mr. Washington was twice a
TRAITOR. He first renounced the king of England, and
thereafter the old confederation. His farewell paper contains a variety of mischievous sentiments."

" Under the old confederation matters never were
nor could have been conducted so wretchedly, as they actually are under the successive *monarchs* of *Braintree* and
Mount Vernon."

" Mr. Adams has only completed the scene of ignominy, which Mr. Washington had begun."

" The republicans were extremely well satisfied at the
demise of the general. They felt and feared his weight in
the scale of aristocracy ; but they found it necessary to save
appearances with the multitude by presenting a profession
of sorrow. It is a real farce to see the manner in which
the citizens at large were treated, in this instance, by both
parties. *The second burial !* But it is impossible to proceed
with gravity ; or to comprehend by what means Adams
and congress kept from laughing in each other's faces,
when they past their *unanimous resolution* to recommend the delivery of *suitable orations*, discourses and
public prayers."

Have not his partisans so senseless [less ?²⁷
Stripp'd our great nation quite defence.

Callender having thus handsomely handled Gen. Washington, attacks Mr Adams in a manner equally masterly. But by further quotations we may perhaps, by the *weight* of our notes, break the peg of our poetry, and fall into the merciless fangs of the criticks. Good democrats, however, with their usual ingenuity, have attempted to wipe away every stain from Mr. Jefferson's immaculate character.

In the first place they contended that 'the report of Mr. Jefferson's having been concerned in the Prospect before us was a " federal lie." Mr. Jefferson's letters however put them down on that point.

They then affirmed that Mr. Jefferson paid Callender one hundred dollars after having read the specimen sheets of " the Prospect" *out of charity*. Finding this ground untenable they pretend that Mr. Jefferson knew nothing of the contents. But it appeared that Mr. Jefferson paid Callender fifty dollars, in part, after Callender had been convicted of sedition for publishing " the Prospect," and of course Mr. Jefferson must have been acquainted with the contents of the work, and that Mr. Jefferson moreover remitted Callender's fine of 200 dollars, when the contents of the Prospect had long been known.

The editor of the Boston Repertory declared that he was possessed of a paragraph in Mr. Jefferson's handwriting, which was incorporated with Mr. Jefferson's

F 2

While Europe rings with war's alarms,
And half the world is up in arms?

own slander in the body of the Prospect " without marks
of quotation." The Enquirer (a man hired to vindicate
Mr. Jefferson) admits that Mr. Jefferson wrote a short
and harmless paragraph and *but one,* in the whole book.
Unfortunately, however, for Mr. Jefferson's advocate the
paragraph which he acknowledges was written by Mr.
Jefferson is totally different from that mentioned by the
editor of the Repertory. But this Enquirer-man is doubtless well versed in what Cheetham calls the " *arts of
able editors.*'

24 When he and Genet had a scuffle.

Genet was *privately* encouraged by Mr. Jefferson in
his projects to prostrate America at the feet of France,
but opposed *officially* in his capacity of Secretary of State.
Genet complained that Mr. Jefferson had treacherously
become the instrument of his recall, after having persuaded him that he was his friend, and initiated him into
the mysteries of state. And declared " if I have shown
my firmness (in opposing the President,) it is because it
is not in my character to *speak* as many people do in *one
way* and *act* in *another,* to have an *official* language and
a language *confidential.*"

25 So solemnly ejaculated?

When Mr. Jefferson entered on the duties of his office

Our native vigour paralys'd, .
That now our character's despised,

as Vice-President he eulogised Mr. Adams, then President, in the following terms, " No man more sincerely
prays that no accident may call me to the higher and
more important functions ; (the presidency) they have
been justly confided to the eminent character, which has
preceded me here, whose talents and integrity have been
known and revered by me through a long course of
years, and I *devoutly pray* he may be long preserved for
the government, the happiness, and the prosperity of our
common country."

This was a masterly stroke of policy, more especially,
when it is considered that Mr. Jefferson, at the time of
uttering this solemn petition was employing his purse,
pen and influence, in ruining the reputation, and destroying the influence of Mr. Adams.

26 Of Washington's administration.

Mr. Jefferson is one of the principal patrons of the
Aurora, and was the *institutor* and patron of the National Gazette, which abounded with abuse against the
federal administration, with Washington at its head.

27 Stripp'd our great nation quite defenceless?

Of thirty-four armed ships, our administration have sacrificed, at the shrine of economy (sold for one-fourth

And sunk in foreign estimation
To lowest point of degradation ?

Plunder'd by every rascal pirate,
Who thinks us mark enough to fire at,
And forc'd to suffer with humility
Insults from Spanish imbecility.[28]

Though democratick impudences,
To merit making false pretences,
Proclaim us prosperous and happy,
Like Stingo with his jug of nappy.

part of their cost) all but thirteen, and some of those which remain are rotting in *philosophical* dry docks. But *economy* is the order of the day, and a *wasteful economy*, is a contradiction in terms.

28 Insults from Spanish imbecility.

Depredations on our commerce are committed daily, by the Spaniards and other nations of Europe (Sept. 1805.) Mr. Jefferson however, has said, that "history bears witness to the fact, that a just nation is trusted at its bare word, when recourse is had to armaments and wars to bridle others." It is to be lamented that these depredators should spoil the president's *fine theory.*

Yet this prosperity they boast,
The theme of many a July toast,
Is all the fruit of Federal toils,
Though Demo's *riot* in their spoils.

What though they boast their knack at sav-
'Gainst Fed'ral waste forever raving, [ing,
Still decency should keep them dumb,
For what they say is all a hum.

In Africk, lo, what triumphs won
Have told the world what might be done,
Did not a weak administration
Contrive to paralyse the nation !

The *Federal* navy overawes
Fell hordes of murderous Bashaws,
From whence each democrat assumes
To deck his sconce with borrow'd plumes.[30]

30 To deck his sconce with borrow'd plumes.

Mareat cornicula risum
Furtivis nudata coloribus,   Hor.

" Stripp'd of their borrow'd plumes, these crows forlorn
Shall stand the laughter of the public scorn."

Thus Duane's Turner cut a figure,
And felt, no doubt, as big, or bigger
In cloak he'd stolen, as if the same
Had been his own by rightful claim.

Why don't our Carter-hill commander,
Who's so beset with Federal slander,
Pursue the rogues who " dare devise"
Against his Majesty such lies ;[30]

The federalists are accused by their political opponents of having been sparing of their eulogies on the heroes who distinguished themselves at Tripoli. This, if
true, evinces the folly and stupidiy of that party ; for
those men, who have been most distinguished by their
exploits against those pirates, were *federalists*, and most
of them commissioned by Washington and Adams.

30 Against his Majesty such lies ;

To show to what an amount the impudence of some
federal newspaper editors will carry them, we will make
one or two extracts from remarks of the editor of the New-
York Evening Post, on Mr. Jefferson's inaugural speech
No. 2.
    Mr. Jefferson, having reference to some tough libellous
truths, which have appeared in the federal newspapers
against him, observed in his speech, that "the artillery

Because in spite of his renown
He knows the truth would put.him down,

of the press has been levelled against us, charged with
whatsoever its licentiousness could devise or dare," and
that " he who has time, renders a service to public morals and public tranquillity, in reforming these abuses by
the salutary coercions of law." Coleman, supposing, no
doubt, that nobody could ever find " time" for attend-
ing to these " salutary coercions," makes perhaps very
true, but very *libellous* remaiks.

Mr. Jefferson in his speech had observed, " I fear not
that motives of interest may lead me astray ; I am sensible of no passion which could seduce me knowingly from
the path of justice." Mr. Coleman comments as follows :
" He, who with the *bribery of office* has corrupted the
integrity of the nation, has demoralized the American
people for the purpose of personal aggrandizement, now
boasts that no motives of interest can lead him astray.
He, who in a publick address to the senate of the United
States, solemnly declared that Mr. John Adams was an
eminent character, whose talents and integrity had been
long known and revered by him (Mr. Jefferson) through
a long course of years, and had been the foundation of
a cordial and uninterrupted friendship between them ;
and concluded with " devoutly (his own word) devoutly praying," that the same Mr. Adams " might be long
preserved for the government, the happiness, and prosperity of our common country," went away and hired a

Nor has he hardihood to sport
His rotten character in court.

mercenary rascal to make it his business to traduce this.
very Mr. Adams, in the most violent language that his
invention could supply.   Yes, he feasted his eyes with
the perusal of the manuscript, in which the man with
whom he had so long, as he told the senate, " maintain-
ed a cordial and uninterrupted friendship," was spoken
of as the lowest of wretches, where he was denominated
the most execrable of SCOUNDRELS, the *scourge*, the
scorn, the outcast of America, without abilities, and
without virtue, and then returned it with the most unqualified approbation, saying, that " *such papers could
not fail to produce the best effect*," and as a part recom-
pence, sent him an order for fifty dollars on account of
previous work.   Need any thing more be added ? yes,
one tale shall be added, and in very explicit language, so
that if the Attorney General of the United States can
" find time," and Mr. Jefferson should still remain of
opinion, after seeing the article, (and I know he honours
the Evening Post with his perusal) that it will be render-
ing a " service to publick morals and publick tranquillity," to resort to the " salutary coercion of law," and
prosecute the editor for a libel, matter may not be wanting on which to found the indictment.   I only stipulate
for the privilege of giving the truth in evidence.   Then
be it known, that he who now holds himself up to the
world as a man incapable of being seduced by passion
from the path of rectitude, stole to the chamber of his

Thus spake this muttering son of slander,
And made it plain to each bye-stander

absent friend by night, and attempted to violate his bed. * * *

" As it generally happens, that when once the devil gets hold of a man he seldom lets him go with a single crime on his head, so this man, to the baseness of his first attempt, added a second. As a cover to the abrupt disconnection of intercourse that followed the disclosure of the secret to the husband, he told a base and slanderous lie, and said, that his intimacy with Mr. Walker had been broken off by Mr. Walker's unhandsome conduct in the settlement of an estate, which he had in charge; all which now stands on record, being very handsomely engrossed with his own hand. Now let Mr. Jefferson, if he pleases, call this a " false and defamatory publication," and recommend a prosecution accordingly."

What a daring fellow this, but nobody can " find time" to prosecute him. Moreover, Mr. Jefferson's vindicator in the " Richmond Enquirer," has made this appear to be a very trivial affair, for he says,

IF THE TALE OF MRS. WALKER WAS REHEARSED TO A NATION OF ANCHORITES, THEY WOULD SMILE AT ITS ABSURDITY; THAT AN INDIVIDUAL SHOULD BE ABUSED, CENSURED, AND THREATENED WITH EXPOSURE IN THE PUBLICK PRINTS, FOR HAVING, FORTY YEARS SINCE, FELT AN IMPROPER PASSION: AT A TIME WHEN YOUTH, EXEMPTION FROM MATRIMONIAL OBLIGATIONS, AND THE FORCE OF FEELING MIGHT BE PLEADED WITH JUSTICE!!!

G

He was a rogue belonging unto
The most nefarious Essex junto.[31]

But should I ever hear again
A scoundrel mutter such a strain,
I'll teach the knave by dint of banging,
A prettier method of haranguing.

For know ye stubborn Feds, that I
Am very nearly six feet high,
Stout in proportion, own a cudgel
For those of Jefferson who judge ill.

31 The most nefarious Essex Junto.

The Essex Junto is one of the bugbears, with which
the Boston Chronicle scribblers frighten the babes and
old women of democracy. But this, like many other
gun-powder plots against the peace and dignity of the
sovereign people, is a phantom which they have conjured
up for the purpose of deception. The men whom they
would designate as an Essex Junto, are as much inter-
ested in the preservation of a Republican government, as
any men in the community, and would, by the intro_
duction of a Monarchical government, dig a pit for their
own destruction.

So say the Federalists, but they are Monarchy-men
notwithstanding, and wish to make John Adams king.

With plenipotent paw a club in,
I'll give each Fed'ral rogue a drubbing
Who wont *humillime* succumb, ·
At beat of our poetick drum,

And kneel before the mighty man,
Who leads the democratick van,
The glorious Chief of Carter's mountain
Of democratick power the fountain ;—

The theme of demi-adoration,
The very right-hand of our nation,
Compar'd with whom, all heroes must rate
As gun-boat liken'd to a first-rate.[32]

32 As gun-boat liken'd to a first rate.

The curious system of Mr. Jefferson, for creating a
naval force adequate to the defence of our commerce, by
gun-boats, No's. 1, 2, &c. up, perhaps, to 5 or 6, is
thus described in the New Year's Message, from the
carriers of the Boston Palladium. Although gun-boat
number one, as there exhibited, may appear to be somewhat too consequential to be introduced by way of *com-
ment* on our *political text*, yet, as it appears to have some
connection with our simile, we give it a place.

And though I shan't have much to say t'ye,
You'll find my arguments are weighty,

Have not our wise administration
Done certain wonders for the nation?
O yes—they've built us more than one boat,
In modern jargon cali'd a Gun Boat.
Yes;—they have built us—let me see,
Enough to make out *nearly* THREE,
But one of those, O what a rare go,
March'd to a cornfield for a scare-crow!
Which show'd Miss Gun-Boat's calculation,
And that *she knew her proper station!*
O did *her masters* but know *theirs,*
L—d, how 'twould brighten our affairs.
    Our Gun-Boats! themes of admiration
To every seaman in the nation,
The very essence, in reality,
Of vast *philosophasticality!*
One round half dozen, I've a notion,
Would carry terror through the ocean,
And eight or ten, in my opinion,
Would give us Neptune's whole dominion!
    Should Britain come, with all her shipping,
Good L—d, we'd give her such a whipping,
She'd wish the navy of her island
Had been just nineteen leagues on dry land
Before she'd impudence to enter
On such a perilous adventure;
For Number One will sink her navy,
In half a second, to old Davy,

Withal, so manfully propounded,
If not convinc'd, you'll be confounded.

Then, as we wish her nothing but ill,
Her petty, paltry isle we'll scuttle,
And since 'tis time th' Old Nick had got 'em,
Send the whole nation to the bottom !
  What mighty matters might be done,
For instance, Gun-Boat Number One,
From Washington descends in might,
With head and tail " *chock* full of fight !"
  Abash'd, Potowmack hides his head;
Neptune, half petrifi'd with dread,
And awe, and admiration rapt in,
Resigns his chariot to the Captain.
  Great Captain BUCKSKIN; please to ride in't,
Terrific Sir, and here's my trident !
You cut a dash so big and mighty,
You've sadly frighten'd Amphitrite !
My sea-nymphs sure have lost their wits,
There's Thetis in hysterick fits !
Take my dominions, every foot,
O L—d! O L—d! *but pray don't shoot !*
  Now gallant Number One, by chance,
Meets England's fleet combin'd with France,
Is soon prepar'd at both her ends,
Stand clear all rogues, *except our Friends !*
Now comes the fleet in line of battle,
The heaven's rebellowing cannons rattle,

By knocking down each Federal prater,
I'll e'en surpass our Legislature,
In bold display of sheer authority,
In *dumb* and *dignifi'd* majority.[33]

    Each smoke envelop'd grand first-rater,
Looks like the mouth of Ætna's crater.—
Pop ! goes our gun, like Pluto's mortar,
Splash '—*there they are—all under water ! ! !*
Not quicker, struck by Jove's own thunder,
Did earth-born Titans erst knock under,
Than these when hit by their superiors,
From Gun-Boat, Number One's posteriors.
    But were it true, as has been said,
By many a wicked muttering Fed,
That every Gun-Boat is a wherry,
Which might disgrace old Charon's ferry;
Still, when Sir Johnny Randolph's taught her,
She'll *keep the peace in shallow water,*
Strike rampant porpoises with awe,
And govern mackerel by law ;
Dog-fishes, dolphins, if they've wit,
To our Sea-Mammoth will submit,
No grampus dare to stand a scratch,
And even a shark would find his match !

33 In *dumb* and *dignifi'd* majority.

The wisdom of our democratick members of Congress.

But now my modest little Muse,
Who drips with Hybla's honey dews,
Her court'sy makes to curry favour,
With Federal gentlefolks, who waver.

Good Messrs. *almost* Democrats,
If you were not as blind as bats,
Before our Chief, your trembling knees on,
You'd deprecate his wrath in season.

No more at Jefferson be railing,
Nor scout the party now prevailing,

was never more abundantly manifested, than in the affair
of their condescending to remain silent, when they had
nothing to say for themselves. There is, unquestionably,
no small share of prudence and self-denial necessary, for
an individual to curb that unruly member, the tongue.
How great then must have been the prudence and resolution of our good democrats, in congress assembled, who,
for the sake of expediting publick business, could sit mute,
and endure to be pelted by arguments which they could
not answer.

Mr. Dana's eulogy* upon the " dumb legislature,"
will remain a *monumentum ævi* of the wonderful wisdom
which was manifested by the majority on that occasion.

---

* *See debates of congress,* 1802.

Although the tail " has got the upper
Hand of the head, for want of crupper.''[34]

The character of this our nation,
'Tis time to place on some foundation,
Which may without deceit declare
To all mankind just what we are.

And IF Americans are jockies,
IF public virtue but a mock is,
Then—" Hail Columbia ! happy land !"
Where scoundrels have the upper hand !

34 " Hand of the head, for want of crupper."

This beautiful simile we have borrowed from Butler.
That author applies it as descriptive of the democracy of
the *body natural* of his hero, Hudibras ; but we think it
happily illustrative of the present organization of the *body
politick* of our country. If the reader, however, better
likes the following simile, from the same author, Butler,
it is much at his service.

For as a fly that goes to bed,
Sleeps with his tail above his head,
So in this mongrel state of ours,
The rabble are the supreme powers.

But let Columbia be contented,
As she's at present represented,
Nor at our democrats be vext,
Lest their great prototype come next.

Now I'm a man, who would not keep ill
Terms, with my sovereign friends, the
 people,
Have therefore strove with main and might
To wash their Ethiopian white.

That I might suit them to a tittle,
Have stretch'd the truth—and lied a little,
For which, my complaisance, I beg,
They'll hoist my bardship up a peg

Or two or so, for I've a notion
That none can better bear promotion,
And I'll accept of any thing
From petty juryman to king.

Besides, I fancy that his highness
Wont treat his eulogist with shyness,
But compliment me with a pension,
And fine things which I need not mention;

For Canto Fourth, of this my poem,
Read by his Mightiness, will show him,
He has a friend expert enough in
The democratick art of puffing.

But please his Highness-ship, I wont
Be Deputy to Mr. Hunt—[35]
No, were it offer'd 'twould be vain, he
Wont catch me in Louisiana.

35 Be Deputy to Mr. Hunt.

The appointment of a Mr. Hunt to be governor of a
district in Louisiana, exhibits wonderful proof of Mr.
Jefferson's solicitude to reward *merit*, and *long tried* and
faithful services. It is true, that this gentleman is yet a
boy in years, to say nothing of his intellect ; but his exertions in favor of Mr. Jefferson, have been to the full
amount of——his abilities. Only those who are best acquainted with his excellency, governor Hunt, can appre-
ciate the stupendous degree of discernment, which Mr.
Jefferson has displayed in his appointment.

CANTO V.

THE GIBBET OF SATIRE.

ARGUMENT.

The Bard proceeds in an ungrateful
Task, which is, hangman-like, and hateful,
A gang of hypocrites t'expose,
And deeds of infamy disclose;
And on the rack of satire, stretches
A set of weak and wicked wretches,
Whose inauspicious domination
Portends destruction to the nation.

YE Tories, Demos, Antifeds,
Of hollow hearts, and wooden heads,
In Washington's own estimation,
The curses of our Age and Nation.[36]

36 The curses of our Age and Nation.

General Washington expressed this idea in his letter to
Mr. Carrol. See note 145, p. 168, Vol. I.

Who and what are ye, Patriots stout,
For Freedom, who make such a rout?
Ye are, or should be, men, I'm sure, [pure.
Whose hands are clean, whose hearts are

O yes! your purity so nice is,
The best among you have their prices;[37]
Flour-Merchants, public defalcators,[38]
Horse-Jockies, swindling Speculators.—

37 The best among you have their prices.

Citizen Fauchet of glorious memory, in his intercepted letter, (which caused the dismission of citizen Randolph, also of glorious memory, the virtuous author of " Precious Confessions") has the following passage: " Mr. Randolph came to see me with an air of *great eagerness,* and made the *overtures* of which I gave you an account in my No. 6.—Thus, with *some thousands of dollars,* the Republic of France could have *decided* on CIVIL WAR, or on peace ' Thus the consciences of the *pretended patriots of America,* have already *their prices !* What will be the old age of this government, if it is thus early decrepid !" See Phocion's Pamphlet.

38 Flour-Merchants, public defalcators.

The " Precious Confessions," of Pseudo-Patriot Ran-

The scum—the scandal of the age,
A blot on human nature's page ;
In these two epithets included,
Deluding knaves, and fools deluded.

Step forward now, and " hear affrighted,
The crimes of which ye stand indicted ;"—
Now, elevate your culprit paws,
While " We the People," try your cause.

dolph, are too well known to require any elucidation in this place. Mr. Randolph, however, is not the only pretended good republican, who has been a public defalcator. .

39 Deluding knaves, and fools deluded.

We speak of the leaders of the Faction. There are, undoubtedly, a great number of honest Democrats, who have been led away by the Faction, to whom this line is not applicable. If a man has no better means of political information, than the Jacobin Newspapers throughout the union, he can be no other than a Democrat, although he may be deficient neither in integrity nor discernment.

H

Step forth, Honestus, lank and lean,[40]
With lantern jaws and haggard mien,
A wight, Lavater would decide,
Was Envy's self personified.

Sir, have you any thing to say
Of scrape fraternal with Genet?
And did you, if the truth were told,
E'er pocket any of his gold?

Does the arch Democrat inherit
A greater spleen against true merit?[41]

40 Step forth, Honestus, lank and lean.

This Honestus is a well known scribbler in the Boston
Chronicle, one of the most mischievous and malignant
democratic Newspapers in the United States. We should
say nothing of the man's phiz, did we not believe it to be
indicative of the qualities of his mind.

41 A greater spleen against true merit?

By adverting to Mr. Honestus's writings, with the signature of "OLD SOUTH," &c. we shall perceive that
his demagogue-ship has spirted his venom at many of the
most distinguished characters in the union. He has at-

And though Democracy he founded,
Is he by viler gangs surrounded ? [42]

tacked the clergy in a most insidious manner, and some
of his essays are *better calculated* to do mischief with a
certain class in society, than if they were *better written ;*
as they are addressed to the *prejudices* and *weaknesses* of
the *lowest classes* in the community.

He is constantly criminating the clergy for interfering
in politics. The " People (he says, p. 218, of his volume
of Chronicle Essays) are willing to hear *gospel truths,*
though they may be displeased with *political heresy.*"
And pray what is this political heresy? Opposing the
man with " no God or twenty Gods." Again, p. 220 of the
same volume : " If the apostles had acted as *some* of our
modern clergy do, *they would have ruined, in the first
outset, the whole system of revelation !*" Mr. Jefferson has
here an advocate worthy of himself!

I think I can in no way express the reasons why the
clergy ought to exert themselves in opposition to Mr.
Jefferson, more forcibly than by presenting my readers
with the following extract from remarks on the Thanks-
giving Sermon of Mr. Parish, by the Editor of the Boston Repertory.

" It is true, the President of the United States, and
the clergy of our country are at variance; but the controversy is not on subjects of politics, on forms of government, or measures of administration. The clergy
have not " quit their proper character, to assume wha
does not belong to them." It is their misfortune to live

Hast thou supported thy life long,
One measure not precisely wrong,

in an age, when a man is promoted to the chief magistracy of the nation, who has wantonly assaulted the religion
of our fathers, and treated those doctrines with contempt,
which christianity teaches us are essential to human felicity. It is Mr Jefferson who has left the character of the
civilian, who has sported with the principles of our religion, and no alternative is left for the watchmen of the
christian faith, but to retreat before his baleful influence,
and apostatize from the injunctions of their divine teach-
er, or to step forth like faithful soldiers, and repel the
scoffs, the sneers, and sophistry of the assailant. The
elevated station of Mr. Jefferson, so far from imposing an
obligation of silence, calls on the clergy for a more zealous exertion of their powers in defence of religion, in
proportion as his writings are like to possess greater weight
from his political ascendance."

12 Is he by viler gangs surrounded?

We do not pretend to give a history of Honé's private
Jockey-club. Suffice it to say, that the nefarious renegade, Pasquin, is one of his privy counsellors, and he
alone is a gang.

Since writing the above, Pasquin has relinquished the
service of the Boston Chronicle, in which he and Honestus were Co-editors. [Oct. 1805]

One single thing, when you your best did,
Whose usefulness by *time* is tested ?⁴³

When did the tyrant Bonaparte,
E'er find an advocate more hearty ?
Or one more ready to advance .
The wildest whims of frantick France ?⁴⁴

43 Whose usefulness by *time* is·tested.

This observation does not apply, exclusively, to the demagogue now under consideration. None of those measures, of which democrats have been such strenuous advocates, have been found of practical utility ; and since they have been in power, they have copied the example of the federalists, except in certain measures, which are calculated to oppress the poorer people ; such as repealing taxes on carriages, loaf-sugar, and other luxuries, and increasing them on salt, and other necessaries of life.

44 The wildest whims of frantick France?

A review of the scrawl of this, and other Chronicle patriots, on the subject of the French revolution, ever recalls to memory, the following lines from Cowper:

> " Yon roaring boys, who rave and fight
>   On t'other side th'Atlantick,
> I always thought were in the right,
>   But most so, when most frantick."

Are you the Jacobin of spirit,
Who first *found out* your own great merit,
And in political careering,
First practis'd *self-electioneering* ?[45]

How came you, modest Sir, to hit on
This horrid practice of Great Britain,
When you, as every body knows,
Are one of her determin'd foes?

Are you indeed the very man,
Who *seem'd* t' oppose the Funding Plan,
An hypocritical pretence
To pocket its emoluments ?[46]

45 First practis'd *self-electioneering* ?

We believe Honestus is the personage who introduced
in Massachusetts that appendage of British corruption,
self-electioneering. He first mounted the hustings, West-
minster-like, and told all the world *what nobody knew before,* that he was *himself* a very proper candidate for office, a friend to the people, &c.

46 To pocket its emoluments'?

Honestus was once a very strenuous opponent to the funding system. Now, forsooth, as Commissioner of Loans,

Has it not been your constant aim,
The passions of the mob t' inflame;
Their jealousy and pride exciting
By flattery, falsehood, and backbiting?[47]

he is pocketing the people's money, in consequence of
holding an office, which is an appendage of the same *once*
obnoxious system. What a pure patriot ! †

47 By flattery, falsehood, and backbiting?

We have but one simple apology to make for taking
notice of " OLD SOUTH," alias " Honestus." In this
apology we beg leave to repeat a sentiment which we have
before expressed, that the *bite of an asp* may be as fatal
as the *paw of a lion.*   Old South's writings would be esteemed by us as too insipid for animadversion, were they
not calculated, by virtue of that same insipidity, to be
very mischievous.   He never soars above the level of the
understanding of the lowest class of the community, and
like a fanatical preacher, his essays are always addressed
to the passions and the feelings of those men, whose passions and feelings are· *strong*, but whose intellects are
weak, and who are the soul of all those violent revolutions,
which leave society worse than they found it.
   " OLD SOUTH" is ever harping on the subject of the
" BENEVOLENCE AND THE DIGNITY OF THE PEO-
PLE." It would be very well to recommend those virtues, and to suppose that they do exist in a high degree
in America, as this supposition may do something to-

Pray Sir, if one may be so bold,
How many lies may you have told,

wards forming a NATIONAL CHARACTER among Americans, and lead to a high sense of honor and honesty, without which there can be no real freedom, or long continued national prosperity. But what conclusions does Mr. OLD SOUTH draw from his premises under that head? That if the people were left destitute of restraints, by enjoying liberty without law, all would be "BENEVOLENCE and DIGNITY". But the experience of all ages is against him. A purely *democratick* government would soon be a *savage state.**

"OLD SOUTH," in a long essay on the subject of " the benevolence and dignity of the people," produces one extraordinary instance of democratick insanity, in proof of his assertions : " As soon," says he, " as peace was proclaimed between the two nations, (France and England) the people exercised their *natural benevolence,* and rushed forth like a torrent, to receive with open arms, the messenger of this joyful intelligence ; the city of London resounded with " long live Bonaparte ! long live the French nation ! the horses were dismissed from the carriages, as being too slow in their progress, and the people became the promulgators of the glad tidings, by conducting the herald to the metropolis."

Here is Hone's specimen of. " BENEVOLENCE AND DIGNITY." These *biped coach-horses* of Mr. Lauriston,

---

* See *note* 29. *p.* 21, *Vol.* I.

Since you, and certain other knowing
Knaves, set the Chronicle a going?

Now, ere too late, begin repentance,
Before the people pass their sentence,
That they no longer will be bit
By such a shallow hypocrite.[48]

exhibited much *democratick* dignity in their silly manœuvre of dragging this " herald of peace," to St. James's
palace.   But what said those who *knew something* of this
subject? That the peace was hollow, insincere on the
side of Bonaparte, and that England must arm, and be on
the alert, or submit to the domination of that unprincipled usurper.

   This is an instance among a thousand, of Hone's incon-
sistencies.   The man is wrong-headed ; he has furnished
his noddle with a jumble of facts and principles, but has
not sufficient strength of intellect to digest, and draw proper conclusions from the things which come within the
sphere of his knowledge.   A *" little learning,"* with a
great deficit of common sense, makes a man very mischievous in society.

   48 By such a shallow hypocrite.

We are not fond of calling names, but it sometimes becomes necessary for a right understanding of things.
That Mr. Honestus has endeavoured to make his patriot-

For though you stride, without remorse,
Fell faction's hobbling hobby horse,

ism a stepping-stone to power, is evident from his conduct, which has not been quite so equivocal as his professions.

Mr. Honestus pretends to rank himself with the patriots of 1775, and anathematizes all those who will not pronounce his Shibboleth, as old tories. But unless we are
wrongly informed, this gentleman, during our revolutionary war, although perhaps not in a cave, sought an asylum in obscurity. He began, however, to fish in the
troubled waters, which succeeded the revolution, about
the time of Shays' insurrection, and has been ever since
constant in his efforts to arm the *passions* against the *intellect* of the community, and set the *physical*, in battle
array against the *intellectual* powers of society.

The motives of Honestus in such proceedings, are
probably, similar to those of all other demagogues. Pride
and ambition impel him to strive to be a great man.
But nature having been somewhat niggardly with regard
to those endowments, which, in regular governments, are
thought necessary to qualify a man for office, Honestus
has no other way of gratifying his leading propensity,
than to excite confusion, in order to rise in the tumult.
But, notwithstanding all his canting about his friendship
to the people, we have never heard of his hesitating to
pocket their money, even for services in those offices
which he had stigmatised as burthensome and expensive.
A fig for such a friend to the people!

The jade may toss, by sudden flirt,
Your demagogue-ship in the dirt.[49]

For freedom you may make a pother,
But 'twill be known, one time or other,
How oft the People's good is lost in
The greater good of Mr.——

Step forward, " simple" Tony Pasquin,[50]
In Presidential favour basking,[51]

49 Your demagogue-ship in the dirt.

" So have I seen with armed heel,
A wight bestride a common-weal,
While still the more he kick'd and spurr'd,
The less the sullen jade has stirr'd."
HUDIBRAS, *Canto* I.

50 Step forward, " simple" Tony Pasquin.

This reptile, who is the right hand Chronicle-man,
has been so pre-eminently infamous, that it appears there
was put one step which the creature could take to complete the degradation of his character, to the lowest pitch
of which human nature is capable. This step he has
taken, by enlisting into the Chronicle service, and exerting himself to diffuse the poison of his principles among

A very ,proper sort of crony,
For such a wight as Mr. Honé

the poor deluded beings, who are so simple as to reap
the effusions of his " jobbernow!."

We shall not here attempt, what we once intended, a
sketch of his biography, but merely state a few particu-
lars, which will be evincive of the kind of talents, which
are necessary to qualify a man for the eminent station of
Editor of a democratic Newspaper.

In Tony's celebrated law-suit against Faulder and
others, which has been published in the Repertory in this
town, and which we remember to have seen in England,
there appears such a developement of the infamy of this
most detestable of all wretches, that one would not
think it possible, that a 'human being, who possessed the
least pretensions to respectability in society would be his
associate.

I will not trouble the reader with any minute strictures
on the character of this pitiful vagrant, but merely conclude this note with the concluding remark of Mr. Garrow, in the trial to which I have above referred, together
with a statement of the result of the trial, in which this
pure-hearted patriot sought recompense for having been
calumniated.

" I see by your countenances, gentlemen, that it is
unnecessary to proceed any further with this man's infamous and abominable productions. I will not, therefore,
harrass your feelings; let them rest for the present—but
I will appeal to your sense of propriety, to that of all

I'm free to own, that I'm amaz'd,
Your heart deprav'd, your noddle craz'd,[53]
That even our leaders of sedition,
Should *use* you for a politician.

who hear me, and ask, whether this common libeller, this vile traducer of honour and integrity, this hireling blaster of youth and innocence, should be suffered to come into this court, and ask satisfaction for being described under the character he has voluntarily and ostentatiously assumed? Should he, who has been proved before you to be the author of works, of which every line is calumny, sue for your protection, under the pretence that he is calumniated? Shall he say to you, gentlemen, I have been, from my youth up, earning a scandalous subsistence by vilifying my sovereign, insulting his august family, belying his ministers, traducing his courts of justice and subjects, from the highest to the lowest; give therefore, ample damages, because this dirty occupation is not sufficiently profitable?

" Shall he say, I have violated the ear of modesty in my writings, I HAVE RIDICULED THE ORDINANCES OF OUR HOLY RELIGION, I HAVE BLASPHEMED——"

Here some of the jury got up, and Lord Kenyon desired Mr. Garrow to stop, that more was evidently unnecessary.

He then said, that it was their duty to consider whether the author of such works as they heard read and described, had a right to call for damages.

Our Yankey-Statesmen put to school,
To such a sorry sort of tool,

" With what face (continued his lordship) can this fellow find fault with the publication of the 'defendant, when it appears that the passage here libelled, attaches to him merely as Anthony Pasquin, a name which he has prefixed to writings of the most *infamous nature ?** It appears to me that the author of the Baviad, has acted a very meritorious part in exposing this man ; and I most earnestly wish and hope that some method will, ere long, be fallen upon to prevent *all such unprincipled and mercenary wretches* from going about, unbridled in society to the great annoyance and disquietude of the public."

The jury, without a moment's hesitation, nonsuited the plaintiff, and the audience " hissed him out of Court."

52 In Presidential favour basking.

We have good authority for asserting, that this *fine writer*, received a very handsome douceur from Mr. Jefferson, for his services in puffing the Notes on Virginia.

---

* *Among other stupid productions of Tony, which were read on this occasion, was his Pin-Basket for the Children of Thespis. In this he thus speaks of the celebrated Edmund Burke :*

——" And—Mun, with his mouthful of Christ!!"
Horrid wretch!

Who can't write English if he dies,[54]
Will, doubtless, turn out wondrous wise !

With such a dirty wretch as Tony,
Who but Honestus would be crony?
And what vile renegade but Tony,
Would be the intimate of Hone?

53 Your heart deprav'd, your noddle craz'd.

We have seen sundry specimens of Tony's " admired performances," as he calls them, which were so stu-
pidly wild, unmeaning, and unintelligible, that we have
thought with Mr. Gifford, in a similar case, that nothing
could match them short of a " transcript from the dark-
ened walls of Bedlam."

54 Who can't write English if he dies.

Mr. Garrow has justly said of Tony, that his English
was as incorrect as his conduct.

This paltry scribbler, since the above was written, has
quitted the Chronicle service, after grumbling a few ana-
thema respecting the small encouragement afforded him
in his labours in the cause of republicanism. What we
have written, however, will serve to show what sort of beings constitute the best of democratick newspaper editors,

Your friends, the Feds, are much delighted
To see such noble souls united,
And when death threatens *squally weather*
They hope e'en then you'll, *hang together!*

Come forward, *spitting* Mathew Lyon,
Thy flaming wooden sword pray tie on,[54]

and stand as a monument of infamy against the party
in whose service such a notable advocate was retained;
and in whose service he would, probably, have continued
his *meritorious* exertions, had not the voice of *publick
contempt* fairly hooted him from the scene of action.

54 Thy flaming wooden sword pray tie on.

A wooden sword is said to have been presented to this
warrior, who is alike renowned in the cabinet and in the
field, as a *tribute of respect* for having *prudently* retreated
from a post, where it is not impossible he might have
been killed or taken by the enemy, had he remained.
General Gates, however, like an old aristocrat, ordered
our Irish Fabius to be drummed out of camp for cow-
ardice.

Hold up thy head, man, don't be frighted,
A bolder warrior ne'er was knighted.

Great Hero of Ticonderogue,
So long as valour is in vogue,
Thy name and merits shall be shouted,[55]
Nor once by *infamy* be scouted.

Thou shalt be held in more repute
Than fam'd Calig'la's Consul brute ;

---

55 Thy name and merits shall be shouted..

We are extremely solicitous to eulogise this wonderful
warrior, and have even gone so far as to hammer out a song,
in the prettiest stile imaginable, for no other purpose than
to celebrate, and, if possible, to perpetuate the achieve-
ments of our Hibernian hero. Although we are not addicted to he very vociferous on the theme of our own
praises, still we must beg leave to observe, that in our
opinion, the following song has more delicacy, sweetness,
sense, sensibility, &c. &c. than all the sonnets of Miss
Charlotte Smith put together, and we recommend it to
be sung by way of catch, glee, sonata, &c. &c. at all
the meetings of good democrats, assembled in self-creat-
ed constitutional societies, or midnight electioneering caucusses, ox-roasting junkets, &c. &c. &c.

Or mighty Mammoth, prairie dog,
Or the best educated hog.

THE DAGON OF DEMOCRACY,

A BRAN NEW SONG.

[Tune—"*O Cupid Forever.*"]

O COME let us praise
In beautiful lays,
   A wonderful idol of party,
And each Democrat,
Shall laud Mister Pat,
   The Wooden Sword hero so hearty.

CHORUS

O then ye are lucky,
Good men of Kentucky,
   To choose spitting Matt. for your idol ;
Come frolic and caper,
By the blaze of his taper,*
   And sing, fol de rol, diddle di dol.

No Commandment you break,
Though an Idol you make,
   Of the ugly, old Democrat, seeing

---

* '*Thereby hangs a tale.*'

Duane and thou at loggerheads,[56]
Make fine amusement for the Feds,

That nothing at all, Sirs,
Flies, walks, swims or crawls, Sirs,
   In the likeness of such an odd being,
    O then ye are lucky, &c.

'Tis said that he brags
How one pair of stags,
   Erst paid for his passage from Europe;
But the price of a score,
Would scarce send him o'er,
   And pay for his hangman a new rope!*
    O then ye are lucky, &c.

When our Independence
He strove to defend once, –
   Great Britain look'd blue at his wrath; Sirs!
But Gun-powder's smell,
Didn't suit him so well,
   So he's knight of the dagger of Lath, Sirs.
    O then ye are lucky, &c.

---

* *We mention this circumstance to shew that the price of the beast has risen. When he first landed in this country, he was sold to a Mr. Hugh Hanna, of Litchfield, in Connecticut, for a pair of steers.*

And all good men are overjoy'd,
To see such patriots thus employ'd.

  When once he was bor'd,
  'Bout his fine wooden sword,
   He show'd what resentment is fitting,
  For the sturdy old Pat,
  Like a rampant ram-cat,
   Even vented his venom by spitting !
    O then ye are lucky, &c.

  To be sure he does right,
  Is very polite,
   Whenever affronted, to drive a
  Great quid of tobacco,
  In foik's faces, whack-o,
   And porringers full of saliva !
    O then ye are lucky, &c.

  Though he did not budge ill,
  To 'scape from the cudgel,
   What time a feil Yankey beset him;
  No doubt with the tongs,
  He'd righted his wrongs
   Provided the Yankey had let him !
    O then ye are lucky, &c.

  Although it be true,
  That search the world through
   No uglier beast can be found, Sirs !

And thou hast well contriv'd to win,.
The heart of Goodman Gallatin,.

Good L—d, what of that ?
He's a fine Democrat ;
  And health to the brute shall go round, Sirs !
  And O ye are lucky,
  Good men of Kentucky,
    To choose such a brute for your idol ,.
  Come frolick and caper,
  By the blaze of his taper,
    And sing, fol de rol, diddle di dol.

56 Duane and thou at loggerheads.

This pair of paddies have lately attacked each other
with no small degree of virulence. Lyon, (the less ferocious beast of the two) by turning States' evidence. has *brought out* his friend Duane, and given some
characteristick sketches of *himself* and party, which cannot fail to amuse all those who can contemplate the
backside of human nature with complacency. Had not
the tail of the body politick in America, got the up-
perhand, and as Butler says, "sergeant bum invaded
shoulders," we would turn with disgust from such exhibi-
tions of enormity as are presented to view by the falling-
out of these rogues among themselves. But as they have
a more intimate acquaintance with each other's projects
than honest men can have, it may not be bad policy to

And I've no doubt, but he would pleasure
With all the money in the treasury.[57] [ye,

attend to their criminations, set a thief to take a thief, and
pardon a few who will be active in convicting the rest.

Lyon has lately addressed a letter to Duane, which
perfectly bewrays the character of both these turbulent
demagogues; and if Americans will hereafter be duped by
such unprincipled wretches, they will *deserve* to be doom-
ed to slavery. A short extract or two from Lyon's letter,
will show what sort of a tool Duane is supposed to be,
by his own party, and what honest *means* those in power
have employed, in order to aggrandize themselves at the
expense of the country.

After comparing Duane to a " *skunk,*" and declaring
him to be a " *would-be tyrant,*" he proceeds as follows:
" A wretch (to wit, Duane) hunted for his crimes, from
Asia to Africa, from Africa to Europe, from Europe to
America, landed on the Atlantick shore of the United
States, seven or eight years ago, incapable of earning
his bread, by common honest laborious industry, poor
and pennyless, driven for his petulence from the station
which first offered him subsistence in America, when a
ragged vagabond, with a downcast guilty look like Cain,
expecting every man's hand to be raised against him;
bemired with filth, and shunned as a spectre; with no
other distingnishing property than that of ability to
write with severity; *to give falsehood and lies some semblance of truth, and to give truth the appearance of falsehood.* The democrats of this country were taken in by

'Tis said by some, O far fam'd Matt,
Although a noted Democrat,

him ; by their countenance and indulgence, he became
the conductor of a press, which had been distinguished
for its correct course : they enabled him to put on a clean
shirt, to fill his belly, to look a little sleek and hold up
his head. * * *

" I told the members (of Congress) to give the man
money, all you can afford—let us support him through
the crisis, and if our party succeeds in obtaining the reins
of the government, the paper will support itself; if we
fall, it must fall."

" I foresaw, his charges would be made up, something
like those made for printing for the house of representatives of the United States, which the committee of that
house, with all their vigilance, have not been able to re
duce, nearer than 30 per cent. to what other people will
now do it for, when the lowest bidder has the work."

" I often told my republican friends, in those days,
that the LIES of this man would *injure* our cause, *if*
the conflict *lasted long enough to have them exposed.* A
thousand times has he brought a blush on the face of the
honest men of our party, when they read his *unfounded* attacks against their opponents ; with regret, the most dis-
cerning foresaw, that themselves would be subject to the
same insults and indignities, whenever they happened
to displease this unprincipled scaramouch of their own
architecture."

Thou dost design to turn about,
And join the fallen Federal rout.

" This person is suspected by some, to be at this
time favourable to the views of a foreign potentate,
[Buonaparte] who wishes to see *democracy* and *republi-*
canism," (very distinct things by the way) " wrote
down and brought into disgrace in this country, &c. &c."

Thus spake the valorous knight of the wooden sword ;
but he still remains the very good friend of this "*unprin-*
cipled scaramouch," and, tells Duane " although a provok-
ed monitor, still your old friend is not your enemy,"
That " his republican friends think highly of Duane's
services." &c.

One would suppose, that if Lyon had the least symp-
toms of returning honesty, he would not continue to support a man, whom he declares to " be a wretch hunted
for his crimes from Europe to Africa," &c. and whose
claims for patronage, consist altogether " in ability to
write with severity ; *to give falsehood and lies some*
semblance of truth, and to give truth the appearance of
falsehood ;" one that he suspects to be " favourable to
the views of a foreign potentate," &c. &c. And that his
party would not feel proud in having employed, and
continuing to employ, an " unprincipled wretch, whose
LIES, they were told, would injure their cause." But
like masters like man. They are all democrats, they
are all shuffling demagogues.

And wouldst thóu condescend, my hearty,
To head the *tertium-quid* third party ?58

57 With all the money in the treasury.

The Genevan evinced his partiality to the paddy, as follows:

The Knight of the Wooden Sword, was, in 1803, agent to the United States, for furnishing supplies to the army. He drew a bill on the treasury of the United States, for money which would not be due for a number of months. The bill, however, was presented, and *immediately paid.*

Mr. Steele, late secretary for the Missisippi territory, drew on the treasury of the United States, for money which was then due to him, under an act of congress, for services performed in collecting the direct tax. The bill was presented, and Gallatin acknowledged it to be due, but would not pay it until all the returns under the direct tax had come in, and the accounts were settled. The bill remained unpaid fourteen months, till the accounts were settled, when the holder called again on Mr. Gallatin. But the cunning Genevan would not then pay the bill, because all the money due for these services was not drawn for at the same time.

The Washington Federalist makes the following remarks on this scandalous procedure:

" The baseness of this transaction is only to be fully understood, by comparing it with the one first detailed. In

K

Demo's and Feds would all be merry,
Fell Discord's tomahawk to bury.

the first, we see a man despised by every person of character in the United States, made the agent of Government, and such anxiety shown to render him services,
and to honour his drafts, that they are paid many months
before they are due.   On the other hand, we see a faithful
and good officer, universally respected and esteemed,
drawing upon the treasury for money acknowledged to
be due to him.   The secretary, instead of paying it,
puts it off on frivolous pretexts, for more than a year,
and then subjects the drawer to very great expense,
trouble, and delay, which might have been avoided, by
stating the objections at first.   The damages occasioned
by the protest, are regulated by the different states.   In
few are they less, and some more than 15 per centum
on the whole amount, besides interest, cost, and charges.
A pretty little sum for an American to pay, for the whim
or caprice of an insolent foreigner !

58 To head the *tertium-quid* third party ?

Many of our formerly violent democrats, have become disgusted with their party, and have learned in
the dear school of experience, what was foreseen by the
federalists from the time in which our government was
first organized, that the kind of liberty and equality, for
which they have been contentious, would not be practi-
cable in society.   These gentlemen talk about forming

Thy dagger, form'd of toughest lath,
Would quèll the rage of party wrath;
And, wav'd by thee like conjurer's wand,
Chase Discord's demon from the land.

Next on our list is Tóny Haswell,
But he's so small a thing, that as well
Might giant bold assail musquitoe,
As we attack the puny creature.

a third party, of what they are pleased to call true Americans, which is to comprise all the *moderates* of both parties. This may be well enough, but these true Americans, must become in effect Federalists, whatever they may be pleased to denominate themselves, if they purpose to pursue the real interests of their country. But if their intention is to introduce a new order of things, a system of measures different in principle from those of the Washington and Adams administration, their leaders should be chosen from among the Democrats who distinguished themselves by thwarting the views of those men who laid the foundation for whatsoever of national prosperity we now enjoy. Among these we can think of no person whose courage and conduct so well entitle him to that superb station, as the Knight of the wooden Sword.

Still as his party set him high,
For once, we'll condescend to try,
If we, by any possibility,
Can hit this essence of nihility.

But lest the reader think the topic
On which we treat, too microscopic,
We'll merely undertake to show,
Our gnat-ling in a note below.[59]

29 Our gnat-ling in a note below.

This petty dealer in sedition, has, a number of years past, edited a Newspaper, printed at Bennington, Vermont, which has been as virulent and mischievous, as the limited talents of the *particle*, which conducted it, would permit.

We once endeavoured to give the public an idea of the *thing*, and *its* Newspaper, in the following lines :

At Bennington, a set of fellows,
Of Tony made a pair of bellows,
Then plied their tool, with skill amazing,
To set sedition's coals a blazing ;
And hope by dint of perseverance,
To make all smoke within a year hence.
In other words, the crooked set,
Hir'd him to print a dull Gazette ;

The next great man that I can think on,
Is no less man than Lawyer L——n,
With whom compar'd, your Mansfields,
Are but a set of asses' colts.   [Holts,

A viler and a dirtier thing,
Ne'er caus'd its editor to swing.
His papers, take them as they rise,
Have fewer paragraphs than lies;
E'en Virgil's Fame, with all her tongues,
And many a hundred pair of lungs,
And who with ease, as Poet's say,
Can forge ten-thousand lies a day,
Has brok'n her brazen trump, and sighing,
To Tony yields the palm of lying!.

But quoth the reader, tell me why
You thus would cannonade a fly!
Would not a warrior simple be,
At tilt and tourn'ment with a flea!
We own our error, gentle reader,
And stand rebuk'd for our procedure.
Then, Tony, thou may'st creep along,
Unnotic'd in our future song,
From satire's arrows still exempt,
Because thou art *beneath contempt !*

Tony, however, continuing to swell like the frog in
the fable, we were under the disagreeable necessity of mak-

K 2

Lord how my Muse and I should glory
To paint his matchless oratory,
For benefit of future times,
In *ævi-monumentum* rhymes.

ing a second attempt to hit him, and in our opinion,
made a very good shot, in the following sketch of

The ORIGIN and FORMATION

Of the Soul *of a noted little* Democrat.

CERTAIN sages, learn'd and *twistical,*
By reasoning not one whit sophistical,
Have prov'd what's wonderful, to wit,
The smallest atom may be split,
Then split again, *ad infinitum,*
And diagrams, which much delight 'm,
By Mr. Martin, make it out,
Beyond the shadow of a doubt.

Matter thus splittable, I ween,
With half an eye it may be seen,
That *spirit,* being much diviner,
May be proportionably finer,
Nor is this merely *postulatum,*
'Tis prov'd by facts, and thus we state 'em.

Dame Nature, once, in mood of merriment,
Perform'd the following droll experiment,

But poets, critics, each a million,
And each a Homer or Quintillian,
With each a pen can't set forth fully,
The merits of our modern Tully.[60]

> She took a most diminish'd sprite,
> Smaller than microsopic mite,
> An hundred thousand such might lie,
> Wedg'd in a cambric needle's eye ;—
> And then by dint of her divinity, .
> Divided it *one whole* Infinity,
> Next cull'd the very smallest particle,
> And shap'd the Democratic article,
> That little, d-l-sh, dirty dole,
> Which serves for Tony Haswell's soul !

But, *mirabile dictu !* notwithstanding we thus impaled this insect on the point of the needle of Satire, the puny, cat-lived animalcule is still in existence, and *dashes* in the character of a leading Democrat in Vermont.

60 The merits of our modern Tully.

The idea expressed in this stanza, we have borrowed, with some little alteration, from The Battle of the Kegs.

> " A hundred men, with each a pen,
>   Or more, upon my word, Sir,
> It is most true, would be too few,
>   Their valor to record, Sir."

Not e'en the facund Mr. Bangs[61]
Can equal his sublime haarangues,
When all his eloquence unmuzzling,
He untwists Jury cause so puzzling.

By help of statute, tome and code,
A pretty decent waggon load,
When Sugar Cause he had in hand, he
Had almost made it sugar candy.[62]

61 Not e'en the facund Mr. Bangs.

A notorious Counsellor at Law, who displayed much of
the art of turning and twisting, in the Legislature, in the
famous case of Young and Minns, alias the Commonwealth of Massachusetts, vs. Mr. Jefferson.

62 Had almost made it sugar candy.

Perhaps some of our readers would prefer to have the
story of this famous cause told in prose, and as we are solicitous to gratify the palates of all those who expect en-
tertainment from our Parnassian Restaurateur, we beg
leave to present them, together with the flummery of our
poetry, a relish of roast beef from the Frederickstown
Herald, of September 29, 1804.
The editor of that excellent Newspaper, thus expresses himself of the personage whose case is now under
consideration:

With Common and *un*-Common Law,
In which no man could pick a flaw,

" In the National Intelligencer of the 19th inst. the following compliment is paid to Mr. Lincoln, by a writer under the signature of CURTIUS. " The short period during which he held his seat [in Congress] had not admitted of a *developement of his talents*, but he *entered* the body with the reputation of eminent talents."—We should be glad to know with what reputation he *left* it? The truth is, that he entered the body with the reputation of being one of the writers of a Worcester paper called the Ægis, and was supposed to be one of the authors of a series of *essays*, (if a mass of slander, personal, vindictive and unjust, deserves the name) called the " FARMER's LETTERS ;" this was the only evidence which the public had received of his talents, and with this reputation he entered the house, and with this reputation only he left it. It is true, that a farther " *developement of his talents*" did not take place during his stay in Congress ; but it is not true that it was owing to " the short period" to which it was confined. He remained sufficiently long to have developed his talents on the many important and interesting topics which were each day the subject of discussion. Awed by the splendor which surrounded him, he dared not expose his prate to the keen animadversion of his contemporary opponents. Having just sense enough to practise the maxim of " *vir sapit qui pauca loquitur*," he shielded himself in a stu-

He did so learnedly begin,
'Twas thought his head was Lincoln's Inn.

pid silence, and sat scowling at the eminence which he
had not the power to resist. He therefore went out of
Congress as he came in, with the reputation of being a
weak spoke in the wheel of government.

" Mr. Lincoln was now appointed Attorney General of
the United States, and during the long period in which
he has *held*, we will not say *discharged*, that office, he has
permitted a farther *developement of his talents*, by making
one speech and an half in the Supreme Court.

" The first speech was a sufficient developement of his
talents, to induce Administration to believe that in any
future developement, it might be necessary for the interests of the country, that he should be assisted by other
counsel, and therefore, in the celebrated case of the *Sugar
Refiners*, Mr. Dallas was employed, at the expense of
several hundred dollars, to render this assistance. The
cause was tried at the capitol, in Washington, during
the sitting of Congress, before chief Justice Marshal,
and Judges Chase and Washington. The hall of the
court was crouded with spectators, among whom were
observed many foreigners of distinction, and members
of Congress. The honourable Levi Lincoln arose—one
hand was rested on a large pile of law books, which it
would seem he intended to use, the other contained a roll
of manuscript notes of the case, to which it would seem
he intended to refer. He neither used the one nor referred

First he advanc'd with hems ! and hahs !
" May't please your honours, in this cause,
" With your good leave, I say, as how,
" My point the first, I'll open now :

to the other. He was on the floor about ten minutes,
when having concluded his prefatory remarks, he said,
" I will now inform this honourable Court, of the first
point which I have taken in this case."—He paused, " I
say, may it please your honours," (continued he, after a
little hesitation) and paused again.—The Court listened
with the utmost attention ; the spectators who were at a
little distance from the bar, anxious to witness the event
which this illustrious instance of the *" montes parturi-*
unt," seemed to promise, closed up in a semicircle
around the balustrade of the forum. " And I was saying, (said Mr. Lincoln) I have made a point."—He had
so. He had reached one which he could not surmount.
He told the Court that he begged their kind indulgence ;
that he felt exceedingly embarrassed, and wished a few
minutes for recollection. The Court bowed assent, and
Mr. Lincoln sat down.

" After a pause of fifteen minutes, during which there
was the most solemn stillness, Mr. Lincoln rose again.
He continued to speak about ten minutes more. His
manner was wild, incoherent, and unargumentative,
and seemed to be an unconnected, promiscuous, and
irregular assemblage of words, without the smallest attention to an *ordo verborum.* " I have now come, (said

" May't please the Court—I would say—
    hem,

" Fore Gad I'm in a fine dilemm'!—

" May't please the Court—your honours
    please,

" My arguments are *simply* these :

" Let my opponents do their worst,

" Still my first point is—point the first—

" Which fully proves my case, because

" All statute laws are—statute laws ! ! !

he) may it please your honours, to the second point proposed—I say—the second point which I have taken is
this—I have got (said he) to the second point."—He,
however, was never able to get any farther, and the
Court remain yet to be informed what that second point
was.   Mr. Lincoln was obliged once more to apologize
to the Court for being unable to proceed.   He said, he
felt an embarrassment which he could not conquer, and
that Mr. Dallas would go on with the cause.   A confused
murmur was heard throughout the hall ; it was the hum
of vexation, disappointment, and keen remark.   Some
of the auditory felt chagrined at this debasement of our
national dignity ; some felt disappointed and astonished
that this exertion of forensic eloquence, should have terminated in such a mortifying *developement of the talents*
of the Attorney General ; and others laughed at the im-
potency which they had predicted—whilst the poor Mr.

" That is to say—the matter's here,
" Since I have made this point so clear,
" In favour of my cause and client,
" Then our side's right, you may rely on't.

" I think this argument is pat
" In point, it therefore follows—that—;
" Good Lord, I wish I were a mile hence!"
Quoth Lincoln—but quoth Sheriff---"si-
lence!"

Our Lawyer having found, I trow,
That point the first would hardly go,
Now stopp'd to cogitate a little.
To hit point second to a tittle.

Point first deliver'd, as you see, his
Head was not *pregnant* with ideas,
Therefore to put things in a train,
He sat down to *conceive* again.

I

Lincoln sat down at the bar, and covered his face with
his hands. It would be vain to deny the truth of this
statement; the hundreds who were present can testify to
its truth.

For our great elocution's model.
Having discharg'd his loaded noddle,
Found that he must, let who would scoff,
E'en load again or not go off:

Now having charg'd, he rose and fir'd—
A word or two, which all admir'd,
Then for truce put in petition,
As he was out of amunition.

And after many a tug, he found
That point the second kept his ground,
With most provoking " *oppugnation*,"
To our great Lawyer's grand oration.

But tho he suffer'd sad defeat,
Friend Dallas cover'd his retreat,
And, luckily, by his assistance,
The enemy was kept at distance.

But I by no means would pronounce ill,
Of our great man, as chamber counsel,
Although some say he did not shine
In Callender's remitted fine.[63]

Still his opinion's always good,
Provided this be understood,

63 In Callender's remitted fine.

The following account of the leading features of the case to which we here allude, is extracted from the New-York Evening Post :

" On the 28th of May, 1800. James Thompson Callender, was legally convicted of a misdemeanor, and sentenced to pay a fine of two hundred dollars, to be imprisoned nine months, and find security for his good behaviour for a certain term, " beyond the expiration of his imprisonment." Shortly after Callender had paid the fine into the hands of the Marshal, and after the term of his imprisonment had expired, a general pardon of the misdemeanor, *remitting and releasing all penalties incurred, or to be incurred, by reason thereof*, was granted, and sent to the Marshal. Doubts were suggested, whether, having once received the money from Callender, the officer could legally pay it back to him. These doubts were communicated to the acting Secretary of State; [to wit, the Hon. L. L. Esquire] who, after a delay of nearly a month, replied, that the question had been considered, and that " before a fine is paid into the Treasury, a pardon remits and restores it to the party; concluding with a direction to " restore the money to Mr. Callender," which was accordingly done."

The arguments which are adduced in the able discussion of the subject, a part of which we have here quoted

That when you have it stated, nicely,
'Tis what it *should not be*, precisely.[64]

In fine, I think his honour's law-mill,
Should go by water, like a saw-mill,
For that his only chance, I trust, is
To *chance* to do his clients justice.

But surely never man shone brighter,
Than our said lawyer as a writer,

proving that when a fine is paid, it becomes property *vested*, and that a charter of pardon does not imply restitution, are too long to be here inserted.

[64] 'Tis what it *should not be*, precisely,

I have often thought Pope's sentiment, expressed in the following lines, peculiarly applicable to the profession of law.

" A little learning is a dangerous thing.
Drink deep, or taste not the Pierian spring;
For shallow draughts intoxicate the brain
But drinking largely, sobers us again."

A man who has but a smattering of law knowledge, is sure to steer wide of justice and common sense, and attempt to make mischeivous distinctions between law and right.

Not even Honestus can write better
Than I've seen many a " Farmer's" let-
[ter.[65]

65 Than I've seen many a " Farmer's" letter.

The acute, sagacious and subtle essays, which are supposed to have been written by our American Junius, with
the title of " A FARMER'S LETTER TO THE PEO-
PLE," will ever remain a stupendous monument of the
astute, penetrating and profound genius of *Democracy's*
" *Demosthenes.*"* Such ductility of fancy, such mal-
leability and intertexture of simple nonsense, into com-
plicated and unintelligible rhapsody, was never, perhaps,
exceeded by the mad cap French revolutionary declaim-
ers on liberty and equality. We did intend to have fa-
voured our readers with our critical remarks on these wonderful productions, pointing out some of those passages
which seem possessed of Colossean merit. But as we do
not wish to inundate our readers with a flood of *verbiage*,
without so much as a tinkling rill of *meaning*, we cannot
do ourselves the high honour of making copious quotations. We will, however, mention two sentences from
Letter No. X. the one a *little involved*, and the other not
quite true.

---

* *The merit of this figure, we confess, consists entirely
in its application, for we borrowed it from one of the Farmer's Letters (we forget which) wherein the prophet Ha-
bakkuk is styled " Prophecy's Demosthenes.*"

L 2

'Tis true, he has not much pretence
To grammar, reason, common sense;

"IF there is no sense of decency remaining, none incul-
cated by public teachers; IF no beauties are seen in propriety or consistency of conduct; IF principles of enmity
to public authority are disseminated and nurtured; IF
the precepts of the wisest, and the experience of the
greatest men of ancient and modern times, are held in
contempt and rejected, because they are embraced by
the officers of government; IF their unexamined, and un-
tried measures should continue to be rudely, suddenly,
prematurely and wickedly anathematised by vulgar rash-
ness and sacerdotal prejudice, merely because they are
theirs; vain will be our retrospect on past exertions, or
revolutionary acquisitions; delusive our hopes of the future, and miserable the condition of the present and after generations."

"IF a body meet a body"—&c. or to rise to the
"pinnacle of the foundation" of this subject,
IF a man be like a man, who

"Sometimes to sense, sometimes to nonsense leaning,
"Is always *blundering* round about his meaning."

pray who else is he like?

The next paragraph which we shall select for our readers "negative instruction," is an absolute falsehood.

Speaking of a Note addressed to the public by the Editors of the Mercury, proposing to enlarge its size, and
entitle it the New-England Palladium, our author says,

What then ? his language is sonorous,
And, " We the People," forms the chorus.

What though he flirts about and flounces,
From falsehood into nonsense bounces,
He works for our good like a dray horse,
Or satan journeying through Chaos.

Sure such an Ovid in a Murray,
Wont be forgotten in a hurry,[66]

that " for less, infinitely less, was Lyon convicted, Callender and Cooper punished." To those who have read the note and the libels to which it was compared, any comments on this round assertion, would be perfectly frivolous.

66 Wont be forgotten in a hurry.

" How sweet an Ovid in a Murray lost,"

said the Poet; but had he been so fortunate as to have heard the Sugar Cause argued, and have perused the " Farmer's Letters," he would have ejaculated something very like the above happy couplet, on perceiving the fine writer, and profound lawyer, happily blended in the person of the Attorney General.

Whose every word contains an adage,
Meant to reform a bold and bad age.

We next will stretch on satire's rack,
A callous wretch in faded black,
A nuisance in our " happy land,'"
A sort of junior Talleyrand.

Democracy has not a rogue,
Amongst her dashers now in vogue,
A single Jacobin, or scarce one
More mischievous than this said Parson.

'Twere well had he been hung, before he
Began to print th' Observatory,[67]

67 Began to print th' Observatory.

The following sketch, from the Boston Gazette of July, 1804, is somewhat declarative of the demerits of this renegado Parson:

" The Walpole Observatory is understood to be edited by a broken Parson, who, we are told, was drummed out of a parish in Connecticut. There is no want of candor in remarking, and we leave it to others, to apply the remark, if they think it applicable, that there is no worse

Which would have sav'd an inundation
Of lies, which overspread the nation.

man in society than he who is a renegado from his own profession. When a black coat is too tight for a man's limbs he seldom gets any decent one that will fit them. When the virulence of a man's politics or temper, or the high bribes that a party offers for his profligacy, have induced a person to strip off the clergyman, he is generally found to be more deeply corrupt than if he had never endured the restraints of a good character. Tired of being a hypocrite, he spits, like Matthew Lyon, in the world's face, and says, Shame, I defy you—Faction pay me and I will lie for you.

   " In the most Federal part of Newhampshire, there was, and still is, a very respectable and useful Newspaper, called the Farmer's Museum. The old revolutionary patriot, so well known, Isaiah Thomas, whom Mr. Jefferson has dismissed for his good services from the Post office, is the principal proprietor. To attack Federalism in its strong holds, and to carry the party war into the enemy's country, like Scipio when he invaded Africa, this Parson, who had never seen a Printer's type, was sent every one will believe, *by the Administration*, to print an Opposition Paper, at Walpole, where it was not wanted for information, as there was an excellent paper printed there before. There must be something found to encourage this poor Parson to set up a press, where it is manifest there was so little room for his business. What

For this same Jacobin high flyer,
Is such a Satan of a liar,

could be done for him better than resort to the Administration for a good fat offering, that this Priest of Jacobin-
ism might live upon it, till he could revolutionize the
state of New-Hampshire, and bring in Mr. Langdon to
be governor. For that end no doubt he was sent, and to
cover up from the eyes of the people the intermeddling
of our rulers in the politics of the state, this new comer
was appointed Printer of the Laws of the United states.
But the office, it is understood, was erected for the man,
and for the occasion; for the Laws were printed before in
Portsmouth, and one printer to a State is as much as has
been heretofore deemed necessary, especially when we
consider that New-Hampshire is a small state.

" A needy tool for our great men, was, however, wanted, and must be provided for, and in such a way as to
hide or seem to hide the business—for in truth, saving
appearances was all that was regarded.

" Now we beg to know, how much is allowed to the
Observatory for printing the Laws of the United States.
Enough, we believe, to support a Jacobin press. If we
are right in this conjecture, then the people's money is
taken by the friends of reform and economy, and squan-
dered on a worthless tool of office, a profligate minion,
in reward for deceiving and inflaming the people of New-
Hampshire. We hope the accounts of the Department
of State for publishing the Laws, will be scrutinized, and

He lies through habit, strange to tell,[48]
Even when the truth would do as well :

though the Federal members cannot hinder the work of
corruption, they may be able publicly to expose it. Instead of the press being free to combat error, as a great
man chooses to say we make no doubt the Jacobin press
is supported by the people's money, to deceive them.
It is a servile, base, wicked tool of a Jacobin faction. It
is a bell that never ceased ringing for fire, when there was
none; and now the Brissotiness and Robespierrists are in
power, and have set the country and constitution in a
blaze, at the four corners, the bell is muffled.

" No sooner did this man come into New-Hampshire,
than he began to know more than any body else about
the affairs of the state ; and very busily spread jealousies
and suspicions about the honesty and correctness of the
State Treasurer's accounts. In this he followed the example of the *Committee of Calumnies* in Congress, who
reported against WOLCOT, PICKERING and MC.
HENRY, a number of charges, that even a Democratic
majority in congress did not dare to support. In like
manner there was a Democratic majority in the New-
Hampshire legislature ; but they, more candid than the
Nicholson and Randolphs, did examine the charges and
found them *false.*

" The same Observatory man has stated in his paper,
that the votes for Governor Gilman were a minority. In
this he has been solidly confuted; still, however, a lie
well stood to, he thinks, as good as the truth, and *he stands*

His every paragraph's invented
To make the people discontented,

to it. He stands to it, that Mr. Jefferson is *chaste*—
no poacher in Mr. Walker's family—is a brave man—
never hid from Tailton—is a good christian—as good as
Condorcet or Pain—and breaks out into the most out-
rageous exclamations against the Federal slanderers, who
can dare to publish that such a Joseph for virtue, such a
Joseph Surface for talking about it—such a Solomon in
council—such a Sampson in combat—who so abhors to
shed blood, and so delights to shed ink—such an Old
Testament saint, as his Notes on Virginia attest, can be
nothing less than an American Bonaparte, a *Dieu don-
nè*—heaven sent to be our Consul for life, and our Emperor by inheritance—with remainder over to Mr. Eppes
and his issue.

" A good salary for printing the laws, requires, that
tough stories by Col. Walker, or Callender, or any body
else, should be resolutely *brow beaten.* A thousand dollars a year will greatly assist a man to stand strong in his
faith. This reverend Vicar of Bray will not believe, nor
allow the people of New-Hampshire to believe a word
to the prejudice of his patron, as long as he holds his
office.

" The post riders make their contracts with the Post-
Master General, and it is easy to see that Jacobin zealots
will be preferred. See then how completely the press is
made subject to the new administration ; how the Observatory can be almost forced upon readers, and how the

To raise the restless mob, and shove 'em,
To pull down all that seems above 'em.

Museum can be obstructed. The French is not more
subject to his Imperial Majesty, the Citizen Consul, than
the Jacobin press to Mr. Jefferson.

" We are told that for weeks before election in this
state, the Federal papers did not circulate in some parts
of the district of Maine. Every one can conjecture *why*
it happened, though no one can precisely unravel the
circumstances, and tell how.

" Is it the opinion of the Administration, that the people of New-Hampshire are more easily deluded than
those of Connecticut? This Observatory man was known
in Connecticut, and there he had no influence. Was it
necessary to send him away from home, to enable him to
do mischief; or is New-Hampshire thought to be stupid
enough to give success to a baffled and disgraced Connecticut, Jacobin? For our parts, we believe better things
of the Citizens of New-Hampshire; and as the attempt
to influence them is bareface, and truely insulting to their
independence, they will, we trust, evince at the next e-
lection, that they are as Federal as Connecticut."

68 He lies through habit strange to tell.

This stupid fib-teller hammered out half a dozen falsehoods about a single toast, drank on the 4th of July, 1804.
What made the thing the more ridiculous, and would

M

And he has been at work to plaster
His grand illuminated master,[69]
But time would fail to set forth how well
He daubs it on, as with a trowel.

At length the rogue has drawn a prize,
An *office*, earn'd by peddling lies, [70]
But this said office is at most,
An *exile* to a western post.

have silenced him for ever, had he not been a Democrat,
and ergo, a friend to the people, was, the circumstance
of there being a number of respectable persons in the
neighbourhood, who were witnesses to his falsehoods on
that occasion.

69 His grand illuminated master.

This man, with matchless effrontery, has repeatedly
affirmed in his lying vehicle, in substance, that a purer
and more spotless character than that of Mr. Jefferson
never was enjoyed by any mere man; and even goes so
far in his blasphemous impudence, as to compare this
man, with " *twenty Gods,* or N o *God,*" with our Saviour !!!

70 An *Office,* earn'd by peddling lies.

Mr. G. is appointed Secretary to his Excellency Gen.
Hull, who is also appointed Governor of Michigan.

We have the honor next to pin
On Satire's Gibbet, Gallatin,
(Our Gibbet not his only one,
If Justice always had been done.)[71]

71 If Justice always had been done.

That Mr. Gallatin was active in the Pittsburgh insurrection, will not, we presume, be disputed by Democrats,
if we present them with vouchers, extracted from a Newspaper under the direction of their own party.

In Bache's paper of Sept. 1, 1792, appeared the following account of the proceedings of the insurgents, at
the commencement of an insurrection, which cost the
United States above a million of dollars:

AT a meeting of sundry inhabitants of the Western
Counties of Pennsylvania, at Pittsburgh, on the 21st day
of August, 1792:

Col. *John Cannon* was placed in the chair.

ALBERT GALLATIN, appointed *Clerk*.

The Excise Law of Congress being taken into consideration, a committee was appointed to prepare a draught
of resolutions, expressing the sense of the meeting on the
subject of said law.

Adjourned to 10 o'clock to-morrow.

The committee appointed yesterday, made report,
which being *twice* read, was unanimously adopted:

"And whereas some men *be* found amongst us so far

For that th' imported Financier,
Deserves such destiny, is clear ;
Nor shall the rogue, by any fetch,
Escape us, as he did Jack Ketch.

lost to every sense of virtue and feeling for the distresses
of this country as to accept offices for the collection of the
duty :

" *Resolved therefore*: That in future we will consider
such persons as unworthy of our friendship : *Have no in-
tercourse· or dealings ·with them*, WITHDRAW FROM
THEM EVERY ASSISTANCE, *and* WITHHOLD ALL
THE· COMFORTS OF LIFE, which depend upon those
duties, that as men and fellow-citizens, we owe to each
other, and upon all occasions treat them with that contempt they deserve, and that it be, and it is humbly, and
most earnestly recommended to the people at large, to
follow the same kind of conduct towards them."
  (Signed)   JOHN CANNON, *Chairman.*
            ALBERT GALLATIN, *Clerk.*

Mr. GALLATIN, afterwards, perceiving the insurrection would fail, sought and obtained pardon of General
Washington.   But that he retained his political rancour,
is evident from the dismission of General Miller from the
office of Supervisor, immediately after Mr. Gallatin's
coming to the Treasury, whose offence consisted in his
having commanded a body of troops who were active in
quelling Mr. Gallatin's insurrection.

But no ! our moderate Feds say " tut !
" The man deserves some notice—but
" The *truth*, though quoted from the Bible,
" Against such great men, *is a libel.*"[72]

You, Gentlemen, may think, perhaps,
That you are mighty *prudent* chaps,
But know, good Sirs, as these times are,
The heighth of *prudence*, is—*to dare.*

Go, timid Lilliputian souls,
Whom such a vile old saw controuls,
Go, hide your carcases in caves,
Or sit ye down, contented slaves.

73 " Against such great men, *is a libel.*"

We find many of our moderate Federalists somewhat squeamish in this particular. They urge, that the exposition of the crimes of great men chosen into office by the people, is a disgrace to our national character. But these so very candid gentlemen should inform us, whether our national character would not be more disgraced by suffering such characters and such conduct as enter into the composition of our men and measures to pass without animadversion ?

M 2.

But I'll make, with your worship's leave, a:
Slap at this great man from Geneva,
Who worm'd his way to elevation,
And holds the purse-strings of the nation !

'Tis true, this gaunt Genevan, whilome,
Found this our land, a rogue's "asylum,"
Since which, in public matters, his chief
Delight has been in making mischief.

Was soon an imp of insurrection,
A very Jack Cade to perfection,
And seized the horns of Mercy's altar,.
To save his gullet from a halter !

In faction's cause alert and brisk, he
Was once a champion in the whiskey
Rebellion....therefore was among
The rogues whom Justice might have-
       hung..

And had her Ladyship foreseen
His future management, I ween,.

In her strong noose she'd made his neck
    fast,
As cheerfully as eat'n her breakfast.

By Washington, this rebel, pardon'd,
In wickedness grew still more harden'd;.
His industry and cunning bent
To overturn the government.

To Congress sent, in evil hour,
To head the party now in power;
When mischief was a-foot, 'twas certain
This arch rogue was behind the curtain.

And oft he would the Feds surprise,
By artful, well, digested lies,
Wire-drawn, thro' many a long harangue;.
With all the art of all the gang.

But, whereas, in these happy times,.
A wretch is qualified by crimes
And scoundrel cunning for high station,
HE HOLDS THE PURSE-STRINGS OF THE
    NATION !!!.

Well, if no sages of our own
Can give our Government a tone,
Let us submissively receive a
Set, fresh from Ireland, France, Geneva.

Let us in Congress hear with patience,
The worthless scum of foreign nations,
Threaten in vile outlandish squeal,
To stop of Government " *de veel !*"

Though many a foolish Demo. fancies,
This man's the soul of our finances ;
That we have not a single native
Can rival this imported caitiff.

Pray, tell me, what the wight has done
But simply copy Hamilton ;
Such plodding imitative work
Might be performed by any Clerk.

Thus a poor wretch, with scarcely brains
Enough to walk in when it rains,
May whirl an organ handle round,
And make it all so sweetly sound.

But should the lubber of a Vandal
Pretend he had the skill of Handel,
The very mob would find him out,
And hoot him for a lying lout.[72]

But let us grant, in mere civility,
That Gallatin has vast ability,
And in finance, yields not a whit,
To Sully, Hamilton, or Pitt,

'Tis neither politic nor just,
A foreign runaway to trust,
A treacherous and intriguing pest
As keeper of the public chest.

Indeed I'll bet you ten to one, he,
(His fortune made with Yankies' money)

---

[72] And hoot him for a lying lout.

The idea pourtrayed in this simile we borrowed from
the " Balance," an excellent federal paper; printed at
Hudson, (see an editorial article of Jan. 1st, 1805) Mr.
Croswell will be good enough to help himself to an equiv-
alent from any of our best rhetorical flourishes, and accept
of our acknowledgments into the bargain.

Without a drawback, will *reship*,
And give his silly gulls the slip.

Then, should we sink in Anarch's sea,
Would this Genevan care ? Not he,
Provided he can save himself,
Together with his ill got pelf.

Step forward, Demagogue Duane,
Than whom, a viler rogue in grain
Ne'er, fortified by mob alliance,
Durst bid the powers which be, defiance.[73]

Law, Order, Talents, and Civility,
To thy right worshipful *mobility*   [man,
Must bow, whilst thou, their knowing
Lead'st by the nose, thy kindred clan.[74]

73 Durst bid the powers which be, defiance.

This vile renegado, by virtue of his influence with the
mob, is one of the most powerful personages in the United
States. He is said to have remarked, that Mr. J———n
dare as well be d—d as affront him.

Thou art, indeed, a rogue as sly,
As ever coin'd the ready lie,[75]

74 Lead'st by the nose, thy kindred clan.

The efforts of Duane, and of his designing and wrong-headed scribblers who labour for the Aurora, are ever directed to the purpose of destroying all kinds of distinction in society, except merely such as a cunning man may establish as leader of a mob. The learned professions are the constant objects of his abuse, and that of the advocates for levelling systems who dash in the Aurora. Should his plans succeed, *brutal strength*, and *savage cunning*, will be the only foundation for eminence. Indeed he has laid the axe at the root of civilization, and unless great exertions are made to counteract the influence of that vile vehicle of poison, which he publishes, its deleterious effects will, for ages, be felt in America.

75 As ever coin'd the ready lie.

The man who cannot otherwise be convinced of the turpitude of this and certain other artful Pseudo-Patriots, is requested to peruse certain statements made by a Mr. John Wood, a foreigner, printed at New-York, 1802, relative to a history which he had undertaken to write of the "Administration of John Adams." This history was compiled, as the author states, from materials collected

And, on emergence, art not loth
Thy lies to sanction with an oath.[76]

from the Aurora, Duane's private letters, and Callender's works, and was suppressed by the influence of Col. Burr.

Mr. Wood's statement bears many marks of veracity and candor, and if we may believe him, the Jacobins who furnished him with materials for his history, are the most deceitful of mortals.

" Mr. Duane, (he says) sent me occasionally, information as to characters and events, sometimes couched in the form of history, leaving it to my discretion, whether to alter the language or not. Notwithstanding the active part which Mr. Duane had in the compilation of this history, he is pleased to assert in the Aurora of the 12th of July, (1802) that it *contains neither veracity nor dignity.* Such an observation would certainly have proceeded with more propriety from any critic than Mr. Duane, *for the facts furnished by him,* are well known to be the most false and libellous in the whole book." p. 7.

Again, " All the circumstances furnished by Mr. Duane, in his letters to me, proved afterwards to be the grossest falsehoods, most probably fabricated by himself." p. 26.

76 Thy lies to sanction with an oath.

By turning to the Freeman's Journal, of July, 1805, published by Duane's former patrons and admirers, we

Few good or great men can be nam'd
Thy scoundrelship has not defam'd,
And scarce a rogue, who ought to hang,
But may be number'd in thy gang.

With impudence the most consummate,
You publish all that you can come at,
To make, for discord's sake, a handle
Of private anecdote and scandal.[77]

shall perceive, among other proofs of the want of principle of this flagitious wretch, that he made oath to a falsehood about his having been a *long time* a citizen of the
United States.

77 Of private anecdote and scandal.

In the pamphlet of Wood, above quoted, we find the
following remark: " A man, (to wit, Duane) who has
partly the means of ransacking, in a clandestine manner,
the books of a public office, who did not hesitate to publish to the world the contents of letters, evidently intended for the post-office—who glories in being the discloser
of secrets and the unfolder of private caucusses, ought to
veil himself from society." p 82.

N

Your rogue-ship's object seems to be
On " Liberty's tempestuous sea,"
To set our Commonwealth afloat,
Sans rudder, in an open boat.

'Twould ask some folios to unfold
The various lies which thou hast told,
Publish'd with matchless impudence,
In face of thine own documents.[78]

Here we have Jacobin against Jacobin, and it is to be
hoped that those who reject Federal testimony, will not
refuse credence to their own party.

78 In face of thine own documents.

This wretch continued to publish slanderous lies about
the alledged defalcations of Mr. Pickering, while Secretary of the Treasury, long after a committee, composed
of Gallatin and others, had acquitted Mr. Pickering of any
malconduct in his office. After as minute an investigation as could be made by the eagle eye of party, these
democrats themselves testified to his innocence (see Vol.
I, Note 93, page 135) still this factious cur kept yelping
against Mr. Pickering with as much virulence as ever ! !

Among the Catalines of faction,
None call more energies in action,
And, if not check'd in thy career,
Thou'lt make a second Roberspierre.[79]

79 Thou'lt make a second Roberspierre.

In the Aurora, of March 21st, 1805, are the following expressions, which shew what are the views of this *would-be* tyrant :—

"——They will petition loudly for a repreive—they will stir up every interest in their power to procure their pardon—they will writhe, and twist, and turn—they know THEY ARE ON THE ROAD TO THE SCAFFOLD AND MUST MEET THEIR FATE ; but *that* FATE they will endeavour to procrastinate—Republicans, be not moved by their intreaties.

"They look'd at the tree, they travers'd the cart,
"They handled the rope, but seem'd loth to depart."

These expressions, say the editors of the Freeman's Journal, are " diabolical." They most truly are so, but they present nothing *new* to the Federalists. The Federalists knew from the beginning, where Duane and the faction of which these gentry composed a part would lead us. But Duane, M'Kean and Co. were then all Democrats, all Republicans.

And thou, audacious renegadoe,.
With many a libellous bravadoe,
Assail'dst Columbia's Godlike son,
The great, th' immortal WASHINGTON !30-

—

80 The Great, th' Immortal WASHINGTON !

We shall trouble our readers with an extract from one
of these libels.   Although it has frequently appeared in
fugitive publications, by way of testimony against the daring demagogue, by whom it was first penned, it ought to
be again and again presented to those who pretend that
the supporters of .the present administration were the
friends of Washington.

In the Aurora of March 6th, 1797, this favorite of Mr.
Jefferson thus expresses himself :—

"Lord, now lettest thou thy servant depart in peace,
for mine eyes have seen thy salvation," was the pious
ejaculation of a man, who beheld a flood of happiness
rushing in upon mankind—if ever there was a time, which
would licence the reiteration of .the exclamation, that
time is now arrived ; for the man, who is the source of all
the misfortunes of our country, is this day reduced to a
level with his fellow-citizens, and is no longer possessed of
power to multiply evils upon the United States.   If ever.

Through patriotism's specious mask, all
Your own gang could discern the rascal,
But *tertium quids*, quoth spitting Matt,
Esteem'd you none the less for that.81-

there was a period for rejoicing, this is the moment—
every heart in unison with the freedom and happiness of
the people, ought to beat with high exultation that the
name of WASHINGTON from this day, ceases to give a
currency to political iniquity, and to legalize corruption—
a new æra is now opening upon us, a new æra, which
promises much to the people; for public measures must
now stand upon their own merits, and nefarious projects
can no longer be supported by a *name*.—When a retrospect is taken of the Washington administration for eight
years past, it is a subject of the greatest astonishment,
that a single individual should have cancelled the principles of Republicanism in an enlightened people, just
emerged from the gulf of despotism, and should have carried his designs against the public liberty so far, as to have
put in jeopardy its very existence:—such, however, are
the facts, and with these staring us in the face, this day
ought to be a JUBILEE in the *United States*."

81 Esteem'd you none the less for that.

At least were willing to encourage him, and "give him
money, all they could afford." See vol. ii. note 56..
page 108.

N 2.

Thus the Arch Fiend, the prince of lies,
Assumes, at will, an Angel's guise,
But with a Seraph's borrow'd mien
The cloven-foot is always seen.

Though hunted through so many climes,
A very prodigy of crimes,
Your friends, the *quids*, still love you dearly,
And *spitting* Matt is yours sincerely.[82]

Dost thou remember much about a
Droll scrape of thine once, at Calcutta,
What time, invited to a breakfast,
In noose thou nigh hadst got thy neck fast.
[83

[82] And *spitting* Matt is yours sincerely.

See the conclusion of Matt. Lyon's letter to Duane, his
" old friend," &c.

[83] In noose thou nigh had got thy neck fast.

Duane is said to have set up the trade of a Patriot at
Calcutta, and commenced his *useful* labours as Editor to
Newspaper, by exerting himself to foment a quarrel be-

Sir John, however, on the whole,
Was wrong to set thee *on* a pole,
For such a patriot onght to ride
Suspended from the *under* side.

We next beg liberty to handle,
Another vile, imported Vandal,
A *Hatter*, who, by *intuition*,
Is a most *wond'rous* politician !84

tween the civil and military departments. Sir JOHN
SHORE,* the English commander, paid so little regard to
the *rights of man*, that he merely rewarded him with a
kind of wooden-horsical promotion, which is not thought
to confer very great honour on those who are the subjects
of that kind of elevation. He then sent him to England,
from whence he was *imported*, to teach Americans liberty
and equality, under the auspices of Emperor Jefferson.
Duane says, that he was kidnapped by Sir John, having
been invited to breakfast. But the man is so given to lying, that we wish our readers to place no dependence on
that part of the story.

84 Is a m ost *wond'rous* politician !

We mean no reflection upon mechanics. But a man
to be an editor of a news-paper, in a large city like New-

* *This Gentleman, if I mistake not, is now* LORD
TEIGNMOUTH, *and author of " Memoirs of the Life,
Writings and Correspondence of Sir William Jones."*

But highly merits being hung
For *murdering*—the English tongue,[85]
Though that's among the smallest sins
Committed by our Jacobins.

York, of a paper too, which boasts the patronage of government, ought, together with natural powers, to have
possesed the means of information, and to have superad-
ded culture to native luxuriance of genius. Even a " needy knife grinder," must serve some *apprenticeship* before
he can *set up* for himself. But in our land of Liberty
ignorance may be so qualified by *impudence* and *scurrility*
as to entitle its happy possessors to the patronage of our
first characters in the capacity of News-paper editors,.
and thus to occupy the *most important* and *least respon-*
sible situations in our government..

85 For *murdering*—the *English Tongue:*

Had we nothing of more importance to command our
attention, we might point out hundreds of instances, in
which this Mr. " DAGGERMAN," has absolutely *assas-*
sinated the English Language. Sometimes Mr. Jefferson's *dress* is " TERSE," sometimes he is not " *impopu-*
lar," sometimes we are told " Mr. Denniston, another
gentleman and *me* called on him at his house."—But
really we wish to get the creature off our hands as
quick as possible, and shall not therefore enlarge upon
these minor faults.

To *honesty* he's no more claim
Than *Satan* to a *Christian* name ;
Is no more bound in *honour's* fetters,
Than if he *stole* and *open'd letters.*86

86 Than if he stole and open'd letters.

Somebody once stole two letters, written at the City of
Washington, one on the 6th and the other on the 7th of
December, 1801, by Richard Peters, Jun. Esq. *both seal-*
ed and directed to E. Bronson, Esq. editor of the United
States Gazette.   These letters were on political topics,
and were afterwards published in the Aurora.

Mr. Bronson states a number of circumstances which
seemed to implicate one JAMES CHEETHAM, an English-
man, a hatter by trade, and editor of a paper called the
American Citizen.

The editor of the New-York Evening Post, after attend-
ing to the evidence which appeared against this man,
declares that " he either stole the letters himself, or that
he received them from another, knowing them to be stolen.   In the eye of the law both are equally guilty."   He
afterwards invites this immaculate patriot to either sit
down " infamous and contented," with the reputation of
being a THIEF or to appeal to the laws of the land for
redress.   Patriot Jim. was best pleased with the former
alternative.

Sometimes quite demon-like he swaggers,
And threatens *sleeeping men*—WITH DAG-
    GERS![87]
The very next breath, to be sure,
No man has principles so pure.

And this is renegadoe Jim,
A patriot of the Godwin trim,
A useful tool in party strife,
A wicked, faction's butcher knife.

This man, the tale might well surprise one,
Deals out a daily dose of poison,

[87] And threaten *sleeping men*—WITH DAGGERS !

This true imported, "*genuine republican*," in an un-
guarded moment fairly threw off the mask, and told the
world what kind of treatment his political opponents may
expect, if he and his gang should ever obtain their medi-
tated ascendency. He declared in the Citizen that the
anti-revolutionists deserved to be assassinated " in the
unsuspecting moments of sleep." Can it be possible
that such a ruffian is suffered not only to go at large, but
that he and other incendiaries, of similar views, are pat-
ronized by some of our most prominent political characters.

Most deleterious, and design'd
To operate on the public mind.

The drivel of his dirty brains,
(And Demo's pay him for his pains)
Spins from his jobbernowl, and then
Displays it in the " Citizen."

For that is what he calls the paper,
Where he and faction huff and vapour,
But 'tis a *sink of defamation,*
A *slaughter-house of reputation.*

If it should suit his matter's " gestion,"
We'll put Sir Daggerman a question
Or two, that he may shew how fair
A character, some folks should bear.

Pray Jim. didst ever know a man
Who join'd a certain wicked clan,
That in their revels, every night,
Against the bible, aim'd their spite ?

And as that fellow, it appears,
Still keeps *possession* of his ears,

Pray Sir, did *Justice* merely *loan* 'em
Or does he absolutely *own them* ?

And, prithee give me leave to ask it,
Was't in a dirty, old clothes' basket,
(Come ! come ! no quibbling, what a' ye
      'fraid of)
Like Sir John Falstaff, that he made off ?

Some say 'twas in a hatter's chest,
But I'm assur'd that *you know best,*
If that's the case, man, no denial,
Let's have the *whole truth* on this trial.

Did my informant tell me fibs,
Of Constables, and broken ribs ?
A man knock'd down, who strove to quiet
A certain scoundrel in the riot.

Supposing half these things were true
Of some " imported rogue," like you,
Should not the vilest partizan
Be quite ashamed of such a man ?

And can it be, this side the Atlantic
A faction now exists, so frantic,
They hire a wretch to print their papers,
Who is notorious for such capers?

Go, get your bread some honest way,
You can. make decent hats, they say,
Go, and thank God you yet abide
Your former domicile's *outside*.[88]

Pray, reader, how dost like this show,
Of three *exotics* in a row,
Duane, and Gallatin, and Cheetham,
Dost think a score of fiends could beat
   'em ?

O ! what a dirty, dirty faction !
What dirty tools they keep in action !.

88 Your former domicile's *outside*.

Patriot Jim was furnished with lodgings at the expence of the Government of Great Britain, as a token of regard for his prowess exhibited in the nocturnal adventure, which terminated in the demolition of the unfortunate Constable's ribs.

O

Worse than the rogues they offer daily
At shrine of Justice at Old Baily!

Let each Columbian hide his face,
And blush to own his native place,
If such a vile imported band
Must govern our *degraded* land.

But now the Muse of Satire bids
Us glance at certain *Tertium Quids*,
Who've run their skiff almost aground,
But lately tack'd for coming round.

Pray, how goes on your caterwaulling
With certain gemman of your calling,[89]
With whom y'embark'd, in wondrous glee,
On " Liberty's tempestuous sea"?

89 With certain gemman of your calling.

The Third Party gentry of Pennsylvania, a spawn from the same litter with the New-York Burrites, have made violent news-paper attacks on most of their quondam friends and associates, with whom they were formerly united in sapping the foundations of the Federal Government.

Indeed, good Messrs. *Quids*, I think,
Unless you ply your pumps, you'll sink,
And, though I'm very loth to say't,
You almost merit such a fate.

But may you only *almost* drown,
Or, if you're *hung*, be soon cut down,
And never feel afflictions' rod
With greater force than Doctor Dodd.⁹⁰

'Twas you, who first afforded aid
To Duane in his lying trade,
But now he strives to take you all in,
You thwart him in his civil calling !—

Had principle enough to hire
Him, for an *ex officio* liar,

90 With greater force than Doctor Dodd.

It has been said that this divine whose guilt, contrition and punishment have excited so much attention, after having suffered the penalty inflicted in England for the crime of forgery, was resuscitated, and lived in privacy a number of years.

Knowing, for so old Matthew tells,
The man was good for nothing else.

Now, since you are the sine *qua non*
Of all the evils you complain on,
It would be Justice to a tittle,
To let such patriots swing—a little.

But as you have some claims to merit,
Have fought the Demagogue with spirit,
For that, and sure no other reason,
I'd cut your honours down in season.

Adversity's the best of schools,
For teaching vain men, Wisdom's rules,
And when you've suffer'd most severely,
You'll see your former folly clearly.

Thus Neb'chadnezzar was an ass
Until they turn'd him out to grass,
And Trumbull's Mack, in air suspended,
Found that his intellect was mended.[91]

Dear Democrats, now tell me, pray do,
How many a Tory renegadoe,[92]
You've rais'd, by crooked politics,
Above the Whigs of seventy-six.

[91] Found that his intellect was mended.

    " As Socrates of old at first did
    To aid Philosophy get hoisted,
    And found his thoughts flow strangely clear,
    Swung in a basket in mid air:
    Our culprit thus in purer sky,
    With like advantage rais'd his eye;
    And looking forth in prospect wide
    His Tory errors clearly spied."
                M'FINGAL, Canto III.

[92] How many a Tory renegadoe.

Among the numerous instances of the unblushing effrontery of the dominant party, may be included their charging the Federalists with having been enemies to their country during the revolutionary war. This conduct evinces that hardihood in guilt, which distinguishes the veteran offender from the mere Tyro in iniquity. It is an attempt to fasten the dead weight of Jacobin enormity about the neck of the Federalists, and to sink the followers of Washington in the tempestuous sea of Jeffersonian liberty. See vol. 1, note 147, page 165.

Yet, inconsistent, lying prigs,
You call yourselves exclusive Whigs,
And oft, with other vicious stories,
Proclaim the Federalists old Tories!

First comes, the should-be hung; Tench
A Jeffersonian orthodox,   [Coxe,
Who gain'd immensity of glory
In the capacity of Tory.

Although, my fine sir, it was thy lot
To be the British army's pilot,
And lead Howe's myrmidons of thunder,
Your Countrymen to rob and plunder;

Since Jefferson began his reign,
The Democratic smoothing-plane,
In spite of all your Tory tricks, sir,
Has chang'd you to a *seventy-sixer.*93

93 Has chang'd you to a *seventy-sixer.*

Seventy-sixer, a cant word adopted by some of our mushroom patriots, to designate the men who first assert-ed American Independence in the year 1776.

Although for treason erst attainted,94
Thou'rt now politically sainted ;.
Become a very proper man,
For Emperor Jeff' a partizan.

Good Democrats reward you now
For services you render'd Howe,
And feast you with the daintiest dishes
Of Governmental loaves and fishes.

Three thousand dollars, every year;
Three thousand precious dollars clear!
The rogues from labour's hard hand
    wrench,
To fill the purse of Tory Tench !.

Next on our list is tory Daniel,95
And though I would not treat the man ill,

94 Although for treason erst attainted.

This tory of the first water, who is moreover a most
charming Democrat, was attainted of *treason,* by the.
Legislature of Pennsylvania.

In name of Justice, common sense,
To office, what is his pretence ?

How dare the fellow have the face
Toc rowd himself in Watson's place,
To batten thus on merit's spoils,
And reap the fruit of glory's toils ?

O ! he's a thrifty sort of *save-all*,
Has wond'rous skill in matters naval,
Writes letters too, which would not sully
The reputation of old Tully.96

95 Next on our list is Tory Daniel.

This man was appointed Navy Agent in the place of
Mr. James Watson. The latter was an officer in the Connecticut line, in the revolutionary war.

96 The reputation of old Tully.

We shall trouble our readers with but a brief specimen
of this gentleman's elegant epistolary stile.

In an official letter to " Gen. Samuel Smith, Esq." dated
New-York, May 13, 1801, occurs the following highly
polished paragraph.

And there's a Mister Consul Erving;[97]
Who is so wondrous well deserving,
That sure his present elevation
Reflects high honour on the nation.

He kindled to our great man's glory,
That brilliant blaze of oratory,
Which gave him nineteen times the odds
Of Homer's stoutest heathen Gods.[98]

"I had the honour of writing to you yesterday, to
which beg your reference. The hasty *result* of my observations respecting a navy yard *are* as follows. The
situation combined has, undoubtedly, advantages for the
purposes intended—one disadvantage most striking to me
is the exposure to an enemy landing in the rear, the *dangers* of which *is* not so great on reflection, and more in
sound than in reality."

The "*result are*" that, in the appointment of such an
ignoramus, in the "*situation combined*" there is "*one
disadvantage*" which although "most striking" "the
dangers is very great on reflection"!!

97 And there's a Mister Consul Erving.

This Gentleman has tasted of Mr. Jefferson's bounty
in an appointment to a Consulship in London.

And dealt in thunder and in light'ning,
And cut a dash so very fright'ning,
And did the horrible such credit,
That our teeth chatter'd when we read it !

He is, indeed, a pretty chip
From Tory block, a kindred slip
A cion from a certain famous
Old Tory Counsellor Mandamus.[99]

A Mister Mansfield takes the place
Of General Putnam, in disgrace,
A warrior whig, O what a scandal !
Supplanted by a tory Vandal.[100]

98 Of Homer's stoutest Heathen Gods.

We have before had the honour to allude to a sublime
specimen of this young man's eloquence in vol. 2, note
1, p. 3.

99 Old Tory Counsellor Mandamus.

The father of this sprig of Democracy was one of Governor Hutchinson's Mandamus Counsellors.

And one old Edgar stands confest[101]
A Democrat among the best ;
What fits him nicely for such rank, he's
Accessory to scalping Yankies.

100 Supplanted by a Tory Vandal.

The cloven-foot of the vile faction was never more completely displayed than in this infamous transaction.

Gen. Rufus Putnam served under Washington during the revolutionary war.   He had grown poor in his country's service, and was obliged, in the decline of life, to migrate into the wilds bordering on the Ohio, and endeavour to provide for a rising family, by submitting to the hardships of a first settler in a dreary wilderness.

Gen. Washington, in order to smooth the path of his life's declivity, appointed him Surveyor General, with a handsome salary.

He was, however, marked as a victim to the relentless tyrants now in power, and the war-worn veteran was displaced to make room for Jared Mansfield, a *worthless old Tory*, hut a *good Democrat.* Yes, this same Mansfield was not only a notorious British partizan, but was active in the destruction of some books, in New-Haven College Library, which were supposed to be favourable to liberty.

Thus does Mr. Jefferson fulfil his promise of " injuring the best men least," and placing the hand of power on " anti-revolutionary adherence to our enemies."

This fine old fellow found the Savages
With implements for making ravages,
Guns, Tomahawks, and Scalping Knives,
For us, our Children, and our Wives.

Not only these, but well I wist,
Thousands might help to swell the list
Of vile old tories, fierce and flaming,
Now democratic honors claiming.

I might include with other lumber,
Judge Stevens, Wilson, and a number
Of such as Harrison and Warner, [102]
For faith they swarm in every corner.

101 And one old Edgar stands confest.

This gentleman, tory, democrat, and tomahawk vender, has been repeatedly honored with the confidence of the New-York genuine republicans, &c. He has been chosen to represent that party in the legislature; is one of the directors of the Manhattan Bank and is in high repute, no doubt, for *revolntionary services.*

102 Of such as Harrison and Warner.

ı William Stevens of Georgia, was appointed Judge of the District Court by Mr. Jefferson. The amount of his

Might swell our catalogue with various
Like idiotic Arcularius,
But cannot stoop in our progression,
To pick up every dirty Hessian.103

But though democracy now glories
In such a wondrous gang of tories,

claims for that station consist, we believe, in his being a good democrat; in his having been Chief Justice of the State of Georgia, and Lieutenant-Colonel
of the Chatham county militia, in our revolutionary
war, and while holding those offices of trust and confidence, deserting from the American service; receiving
a British commission; being attainted for treason by the
Legislature of the State of Georgia. Such are the men
whom our pretended Republicans " delight to honour."
Wilson is a tory Democrat, of Worcester, Massachusetts,
advanced to office by the present administration. Harrison is in office by virtue of an appointment by the
New-York *tory hating* democratic corporation, as a reward for his services as a midshipman on board one of
his Britannic Majesty's ships, during the revolutionary
war. This gentleman supplanted Mr. Jeremy Marshal,
dismissed from office, for having been, as Governor Clinton (then General Clinton) affirmed of him, one of the
most useful men in the American army. These are only
a few of the many instances, which might be adduced to

With many fools, its knaves contrive,
To pass for whigs of seventy-five.

prove that our good Democrats have been, and still are,
hostile to those who were found faithful in times which
" tried men's souls."*

103 To pick up every dirty Hessian.

Philip Arcularius was appointed, by the New-York
Corporation, Superintendant of the Alms-House.   He
is a Hessian by birth, and, during the revolutionary war,
kept a sutler's shop for the supply of his countrymen in
the British army.   We cannot, in this place, give a de-
tail of the particular services which recommended this
man to our Democrats.   To complete the story, it is to
be added, that he supplanted Mr. Richard Furman, an
American, who had served his country, both by sea and
land, during the whole war, and was several times wound-
ed.   This gentleman had been frequently employed by
his fellow citizens in offices of trust and confidence, and
had ever approved himself a faithful public servant and
worthy man.   He had been extremely useful in the office ·

* For a more particular account of the proceedings
of the New-York corporation, the reader will please to
consult the New-York Evening Post of June 25th, in which
the able and indefatigable editor has exhibited in its just
light, the management of this immaculate junto of genuine Jeffersonians and redoubtable seventy-sixers.

They pile their own abominations,
Enough to damn a dozen nations,
All on the simple harmless heads
Of passive inoffensive Feds.

Deprive them first of bread to eat,
And then their conquest to complete ;
They hire the scum of foreign nations,
To blast their victims' reputations.

Tho' Burnet " fought in freedom's cause,"
He's doom'd to Cheetham's Harpy
claws,[104]

of Superintendant of the Alms-House ; but, as he was
neither a Tory nor a Democrat, he was obliged to give
place to the fellow who has the honor of a peg on our
Gibbet.

104 He's doom'd to Cheetham's Harpy claws,

Captain Burnet, another of our revolutionary officers,
and one of the oldest post-masters in the United States,
has been turned out of employment by Mr. Jefferson.—
Here again we perceive the sincerity of Mr. Jefferson's
declaration, that removals from office should be thrown
as much as possible on " anti-revolutionary adherence to
our enemies."

And Spencer, having put down Foot,
Murders his character to boot.[105]

'Tis thus some canibals, 'tis said,
Still spite their enemies, though dead;
And worse, if possible than Cheetham,
Can't be contented *till they eat them!*

As soon as he was displaced, patriot Cheetham began
to open upon him for misconduct in having been in the
habit of " stopping and destroying Republican papers."
Indeed, in every instance where the mushroom tyrant
Granger, has exerted his " brief authority," by a remo-
val from office, we have seen the paltry prints of his
party rep'ete with lying statements, designed to destroy
the character of those they had offered at the shrine of
the Democratic Moloch.

105 Murders his character to boot.

Mr. Foote was another revolutionary patriot who has
been displaced by the intolerant demagogues who are
now dominant. Foote had the misfortune to think with
Washington on political subjects, and was, of consequence, deprived of office, and his reputation afterwards attacked, by way of palliating such an iniquitous
proceeding.

Here reader, is a pretty sample
Of rogues for " *negative example.*"106
Cull'd from among some score of dozens
You'd think th' arch Democrats first
    cousins.

To this vile crew there might be added
Full many a hollow heart and bad head,
And some for infamy as famous,
As any history can name us.

Among the rest, fanatic preachers,107
Your self-inspir'd, and self-taught teachers,

106 Of rogues, for " *negative example.*"

" We do not give you to posterity, as a pattern to
imitate, but as an example to deter.—We mean to make
you a negative instruction to your successors for ever."
              Junius to the Duke of Grafton.

107 Among the rest, fanatic preachers.

We always possessed a violent antipathy to your bawling, itinerant, field and barn preachers; and having pro-
mised them a dose, (P. 20. N. 24) we now proceed to

Whose piety, so dark and mystical,
Is Godward *zealous*, manward—*twistical.*

[108

administer a little of the nitrous acid of Satire, which we
hope may effect a radical cure of their disorder. Our
medicine is as follows :

FANATICISM.

I HATE your hypocritic race,
Who prate about pretended grace ;
   With tabernacle phizzes ;
Who think Omnipotence to charm,
By faces longer than my arm !
   O what a set of quizzes !

I hate your wretches, wild and sad,
Like gloomy wights in Bedlam mad,
   Or vile Old Baily culprits ;
Who with a sacrilegious zeal,
Death and damnation dare to deal,
   From barn-erected pulpits.

I hate that hangman's aspect bluff,
In him, whose disposition rough,
   The porcupine surpasses ;
Who thinks that heaven is in his power,
Because his sullen looks might sour
   A barrel of molasses.

Creatures, who creep into your houses
Just to *regenerate* your spouses,[109]

A stupid wretch, who cannot read,
(A very likely thing indeed)
   Receives from Heaven a calling ;
He leaves his plough, he drops his hoe,
Gets on his meeting clothes, and lo,
   Sets up the trade of bawling.

With lengthen'd visage, woe bedight,
An *outward* sign of inward light,
   He howls in dismal tone ; —
" I say, as how, you must be d—d,
For Satan an't so easy shamm'd,
   And you're the devil's own !"

Fools, and old women, blubbering round,
With sobs, and sighs, and grief profound,
   His every tone respond, Sir,
O could I catch the whining cur,
The deuce a bit would I demur,
   To duck him in a pond, Sir,

If any of the canting race,
Are sent to visit any place,
   Adieu to all decorum ;

With whom the spirit's operation,
Tends to a carnal termination.

To every virtue, now adieu ;
Morality, religion true,
   Are blasted all before 'em.

A good old woman has the spleen,
And sees what is not to be seen.
   Or dreams of things uncommon ;
Yea, ten times more than tongue can tell,
Strange things in heaven, and eke in h—ll,
   O, what a nice old woman !

Straight by the sect 'tis blaz'd about,
That she's inspir'd beyond a doubt,
   And has her sins forgiven ;
How can the wretches hope for bliss,
Who palm such foolish stuff as this,
   Upon the God of Heaven !

Such doers of the devil's works,
Are sure than renegado Turks,
   Worse foes to real piety ;
And though we would not persecute,
By dint of ridicule, we'll hoot,
   The wretches from society.

Your New-York Democratic chickens,
Might make us most delightful pickings,
A very pretty little brood !
For Satire's muse most charming food !

We may, perhaps, hereafter hint on
The management of D. W. C——n
And, though the populace may stare,
May gibbet an intriguing Mayor.

If he and party must have pimps
From Palmer's and from Tom Pain's imps,

108 Is Godward, *zealous*, manward,—*twistical.*

Twistical is a *Yankeyism*, which we have introduced,
by virtue of our authority as a poet *(Poetica Licentia.)*
The idea is borrowed from an anecdote related of a coun-
tryman, who made use of similar terms, in giving a
character to a fanatic of his acquaintance.

109 Just to *regenerate* your spouses.

We have particular reference to certain notable Democrats of our acquaintance, who make extraordinary piety
a pretence for " leading captive silly women."

'Twill prove they're base birds of a feather,
Whose necks should all be stretch'd to-
    gether.

We might allude to money made
By virtue of a Governor's trade,
Might tell the world what kind of barter
Sometimes obtain'd a grant or charter.

Might cut down bankers, rank and file, and
Hang rogues by hundreds in Rhode-Island,
Your patriotic Guinea-men— or[110]
Folks always drunk like G—r F—r.[111]

110 Your patriotic Guinea men—or

Some of the most fiery Rhode-Island republicans
cut of their superabundant regard to the " rights of
Man" are concerned in the slave trade. One Collins
a violent Jacobin, and of consequence appointed a Col-
lector for Newport, is a patriot of that description.

111. Folks always drunk like G——r F——r.

We are told that a gentleman who complained of the
impropriety of which a friend had been guilty, by in

But worlds of folios were too few
To set forth half the crazy crew,
Of sharping knaves, and simple flats,
Who constitute good Democrats.

Besides, for credit of our nation,
We cease a while our *"oppugnation,"*
With these few gibbeted, 'tis best,
Perhaps to respite all the rest.

Some Democrats we meant to tickle,
(And still preserve a rod in pickle,)
May yet escape, upon condition
Of quick repentance, and contrition.

But those most harden'd we'll exhibit,
On this, or something like this, *gibbet,*[112]
Hope yet to hang them every one,
A thing which ought, and shall be done.

troducing him to his E———y while he was in a state of
intoxication, was silenced by a reply, that it could not be
otherwise, for his E———y, when awake, was *never
sober.*

112 On this, or something like this, *gibbet.*

We propose, "till time shall wear us out of action" to continue our strictures on certain flagitious demagogues, who have hitherto escaped our notice. We shall, however, probably publish them in such form that they may serve as a *continuation* to this work without their being blended with what we now place before the public.

CANTO VI.

MONITION.

ARGUMENT.

WE now, with due submission, venture,
To make OURSELF the People's Mentor,
And boldly take the lead of those,
Who fain would lead them by the nose;
And, if their grand Omnipotences,
Have not entirely lost their senses,
By us forewarn'd, they'll shun the slavery,
Which waits on Democratic knavery.

ALTHO' not bless'd with second sight,
Divine inflation, or new light,
Have ne'er, in supernatural trance,
Seen through a mill-stone at a glance;

Q

Ne'er danc'd with sprites at midnight revel,
Had never dealings with the devil,
Nor carried matters to such pitches,
As did the wicked Salem witches;—

Hav'nt made with t'other world so free, as
To go to H—ll, like one Æneas,[113]
By virtue of divine commission,
For prospects bright in fields Elyssian;—

Cannot divine like Richard Brothers,
Miss Polly Davis, and some others,[114]
Who, in the world of spirits, spied
A gross of wonders—or they lied;—

113 To go to H—ll, like one Æneas.

For a particular account of this journey, See Book **VI.**
of the Æneid.

114 Miss Polly Davis, and some others.

Richard Brothers and Polly Davis, well known personages, whose missions and voyages, to the world of spirits,
have caused much speculation among some very knowing
ecclesiastics, whom one would suppose were rather of the
lying, than the *standing* order.

Can't prophesy, as well as gingle,
Like 'Squire Columbus, or McFingal,[115]
And don't see quite so many glories,
As could be wish'd, now flash before us;

Though nothing more than mortal elf,
Good reader, very like yourself,
And therefore shan't, by any trope,
Presume to make ourself a Pope;

Yet ne'er was conjuror acuter,
In prying into matters future;—
No old Silenus, though in liquor,   [er.
Could tell you what would happen quick-

We'll therefore venture to assume, a
Tone of authority, like Numa;[116]

115 Like 'Squire Columbus, or McFingal.

See Barlow's "Vision of Columbus," and "Trumbull's McFingal," in which the heroes of the poems respectively, after the manner of the ancients, take a peep into futurity.

And give such wondrous counsel, no man
Shall say, we fall beneath the Roman.

Good folks, of each degree and station,
Which goes to constitute our nation,
In social fabric who take place,
Or at the pinnacle or base,

With diligence, I pray, attend
To counsels of a *real* friend,
Who tells the truth, when he assures
You, that his interest is yours ;[117]

116 Tone of authority, like Numa.

Numa Pompilius was a King of the Romans, who pretended to intimacy with a female spirit, whom he named Egeria, and whose monitions were probably as prophetic as those of our invisible lady.

117 You, that his interest is yours.

We have before observed, Vol. I. p. 10, that we have no private nor party views to subserve in this poem. We have no *interest* distinct from the good of our country, and *no patron* but the public.

Who hopes, that when you're plainly
    show'd
Your Democratic, downhill road,
Is dire destruction's dismal route,
You'll condescend to turn about.

Why should you hardily advance,
The highway, lately trod by France;
Nor take example, ere too late,
To shun the same disastrous fate.

(O, could I hope my rush-light taper
Might penetrate the Stygian vapour,
That you might see, and seeing miss,
The Democratic precipice.)

But now, methinks, you cry as one,
What shall be done ! What shall be done !
What method hit on for defending,
Against such destiny impending ?

Imprimis, cry down every rogue
Democracy has now in vogue,

Who thinks, by dint of wicked lies,
To cast a mist before your eyes. ·

Give power to none but honest men,
Long tried, and faithful found, and then
You will not flounder in the dark.
Still wide from real freedom's mark,

Distrust those wretches, every one,
Curses denounc'd by Washington ;
Who have of late been busy, brewing
Their *own*, and other people's ruin.[118]

O had we built on that foundation,
Laid by our late Administration,[119]

118 Their *own*, and other people's ruin.

Our leading Demagogues, are quite as likely to be offered as victims at the shrine of Democracy as the Federalists. Governor McKean, who was active in bringing
about a Democratic order of things in Pennsylvania,
stands on very slippery ground, and is in danger of being
denounced by the Aurora-man, who is the Wat Tyler of
the Pennsylvania Democrats.

The fabric of our Nation's Glory
Had never been surpass'd in story.

But ever sedulous in brewing
Their *own*, and other people's ruin,

119 Laid by our late Administration.

To enumerate the most prominent measures of the
Federal Administration, and the benefits which have re-
suited to the nation from the Federal system, would require volumes.   We shall slightly advert to a few particu-
lars, by way of elucidating this fact.

The Federalists found the country without permanent
revenue, and without money in the Treasury sufficient to
defray the necessary expences of Government ; upwards
of seventy-six millions in debt ; the securities of Government selling at two shillings on the pound ; the nation
distracted at home and despised abroad—

Like "some wreck'd vessel, all in shatters,"
Scarce "held up by surrounding waters."*

Such was the state of things when they commenced
their operations.

They liquidated the public funds for the extinction, of
the national debt ; punctually paid the interest and part of
the principal.

They fortified our harbours.

---

* *McFingal.*

Our Democrats have been at work
To lay all level, with a jerk.

Not Satan, breaking into Eden,
Could show more malice in proceeding,
Or tell more false, malicious stories,
Than these said Jacobin-French Tories.[120]

· They sought for and obtained indemnity for British and
French spoliations.

They suppressed insurrections.

They built and purchased a Navy of thirty-six armed
ships.

They secured peace abroad.

They established a Government at home.

They exalted our national character: under their au-
spices Agriculture flourished, Commerce was protected, a
Revenue created without burthening the people, and Two
Millions and an Half Dollars left in the Public Treasury.

· 120 Than these said Jacobin-French Tories.

If any of our readers are not yet fully acquainted with
the despicable means by which our Jacobins attained the
great end of destroying the Federal Administration, they
are referred to Mr. Bayard's speech on the Judiciary Bill,
spoken February 19, 1802. We should be happy to in-

Sometimes the rogues were picking flaws
With Alien and Sedition Laws,121

sert that part of it which relates to a vindication of the
measures of the Federal Administration, did not its length
exceed our limits. One sentence, however, relative to the
clamour, which the Antifederalists have raised against
direct taxation, the abolition of which, according to Mr.
Jefferson's late speech, (March, 1805) is one of the measures so highly commendable in the gentlemen now at
the head of our affairs, we cannot forbear to quote.

" Will gentlemen say that the direct tax was laid in
order to enlarge the bounds of patronage? *Will they deny
that this was a measure to which we had been urged for
years,* by our adversaries, because they saw in it the ruin
of the Federal power?"

This is the way they have managed—cunningly cla-
moured the Federal Administration into measures, which
they foresaw might be rendered obnoxious to the people,
and then took advantage of the odium which such measures had excited? See Vol. I. P. 171 2. N. 170.

121 With Alien and Sedition Laws.

These laws were among the measures of the late Administration, which were obnoxious to the tyrants in power,
merely because they were favourable to the rights of the
citizen. The Alien law provided for the deportation,

The Constitution next attacking,
They sent the Federal Judges packing.[122]

With empty boasts of their surprising
Attention to economizing,
Thousands were thrown away, to show
How they could decorate the Berceau.[123]

under certain circumstances, of turbulent and seditious
foreigners; the latter gave our citizens a right to publish
the *truth* concerning the measures of government. See
Vol. I. N. 12. P. 8.

122 They sent the Federal Judges packing.

No man whose head is not very weak, or his heart very
wicked, can contemplate, without emotions too vivid to
be expressed, the conduct of the Faction in their destruction of the Judiciary. The sound arguments on the one
side, and the flimsy sophisms on the other side of that
great national question, when contrasted, must convince
every person, that those men who laid their sacrilegious
hands on the ark of our safety, were predetermined not
to be convinced, but to stick to their party, right or
wrong. See Vol. I. P. 168. N. 169.

123 How they could decorate the Berceau.

More than thirty-two thousand dollars were expended
in repairing the French Corvette Berceau. The Ganges,

And public money was such trash,
Two million dollars, at a dash,
Without descending to excuses,
Their honours vote for private uses.[124]

The Feds-chac'd down, the snarling elves,
At loggerheads among themselves,[125]

an American ship of war of 26 guns, and all her stores,
were sold by administration for only 21,000 dollars, and
most of the other ships of the Federal navy, we believe,
in the same proportion.

124 Their honours vote for private uses.

See a resolve of Congress of November, 1803, that a
sum of two millions of dollars in addition to the provi-
sion heretofore made, should be granted to the purposes
of intercourse between us and foreign nations.

125 At loggerheads among themselves.

Every body knows that Master Johnny Randolph has
of late been attempting to *put off the monkey,* and *put on
the tiger,* and to *bully* the nonconformists of his party into
genuine Republicanism. But his essays in the *terrible,*
have terminated in the *ludicrous,* for even Miss Nancy

E'en cut and thrust, like gladiators,
For our amusement as spectators.

Resolv'd to prove the nation's curses,
They go from bad to what still worse is;
As females frail, by regular steps,
Are prostitutes from demireps.

Each wicked measure merely leading,
To more flagitious step succeeding,
Of late, their frantic innovations,
Have shook society's foundations.

Hot-headed Randolph's resolution
For cutting up the Constitution,
And that of Nicholson disclose,
The rancour of its deadly foes.[126]

Dawson declares that *she* will not be frightened out of *her
independence,* by this *whipper-in* of the puppies of the
party.

126 The rancour of its deadly foes.

It is well known that the Democratic party were formerly most violent opponents of the Federal Constitution.

That " plague to G—d and man," Tom.
   Paine,
Is at his dirty work again,[127]
The Devil's special legate sent,
And patroniz'd by Government !

Mr. Jefferson declared that he " disliked, and greatly
disliked" many parts of it. We could, therefore, expect
nothing better from the enemies of the Constitution, than
that they would endeavour to destroy it. Some of the out-
works are already demolished, and the citadel is to be attacked the next session, (Nov. 1805.) It is to be hoped
that those Democrats, who are not rendered quite frantic
by the spirit of party, will be taught, from the endeavours
of our Randolphs and Nicholsons, the impolicy of placing
the enemies of the Constitution of the United States in
situations where they can, with impunity, aim their blows
at its vitals. Would any man of a sound mind suffer his
house to be tenanted by persons, who, after having vainly
opposed its erection, had declared that its corner stones
ought to be subtracted from the building, and its principal pillars be laid prostrate? · Yet such is the part which
we have acted in trusting the administration of the Federal Government in the hands of men who were inimical
to that government at its establishment, and who, even
now, neglect no opportunity for the display of their hos-
tility to the constitution by which it is administered.

R

But now, methinks, you cry as one,
What must be done! What must be done!
These growing evils to curtail,
And make our Demo's shorten sail?

Sirs, (our opinion to be blunt in)
The first step must be, "scoundrel hunting !"128

127 Is at his dirty work again.

To wit, scribbling newspaper essays for the Snyderites
at Pennsylvania.

128 The first step must be "scoundrel hunting !"

This may seem very harsh doctrine. The sense in
which I use the phrase quoted in this place, may, however, be explained, by referring to Vol. I. N. 4. P. 4.

I would not wish to hunt bad men with mobs, nor with
mastiffs, but I would hold them out to society in *true*
colours, and if the voice of the public does not consign
them to infamy, Americans will pass from the "tempestuous sea" of licentiousness, to the "dead calm of despotism," with the embittering reflection that they *have
merited their destiny.* Thus, in France, after the destruction of Fayette and others of their leaders, who were
solicitous to reform the abuses of the old government, and
who were mostly well-meaning men, a succession of ty
gers, in human shape, afflicted the nation, till the most
ferocious monster the kingdom afforded, was at length
made Emperor.

The minions of a wicked faction,
Hiss ! hoot quite off the stage of action !

Next, every man throughout the nation,
Must be contented in his station,[129]

129 Must be contented in his station.

There is, perhaps, no pride more preposterous than that which impels so many, in the middle and lower classes in society, to exert themselves to confer a collegiate education on their children, not only *minerva invita*, but when the *res angusta domus opposes* insurmountable impediments to their progress. " What good end (says an English writer) can it answer in these times, when every genteel profession is overstocked, to rob our agriculture or our manufactures of so many useful hands, by encouraging every substantial farmer, mechanic, or tradesman, to breed his son to the church ;" and he might have added, or any other learned profession. " If now and then a very uncommon genius in those walks of life discovers itself, there are seldom wanting gentlemen in the neighbourhood, who are proud of calling forth, and if *necessary*, of supporting, by a subscription, such extraordinary talents."

The multiplying of Academies, and *poorly endowed* Colleges, where that " dangerous thing." " a little learning," may be acquired, and frequently to the detriment of

Nor think to cut a figure greater,
Than was design'd for him by Nature.

common Schools, in which that kind of knowledge is taught which is absolutely necessary for farmers, mechanics, &c. is, in our opinion, a great and a growing evil in America. Happy would it be for us if the number of that *useful* class of citizens, who form the basis of society, was greater in proportion to the population of the country.

With all the freedom you can boast,
You cannot *all* be *uppermost* :

And where *subordination ends, tyranny begins;* at first the "*tyranny of all,*" which soon becomes the tyranny of the few, or the despotism of one. See Vol. I. P. 6. N. 8.

In the general scramble for political distinction, which takes place in America, in consequence of the door of office being open to every pretender, the basest means are resorted to, and the morals of the people are corrupted by the example of those who are aspiring to take the lead in the community. This evil might, in a great degree, be remedied by lessening the number of competitors for offices. Let every man have a right to aspire to the highest stations, but let the pre-requisite qualifications, respecting age, education, talents, citizenship, but above

No tinker bold with *brazen* pate,
Should set himself to *patch* the.State,¹³⁰

all *morals*, be such, that the number of competitors would
be comparatively few.

Regulations of that kind would be perfectly consistent
with freedom, the ascendency of virtue and talents and
the experience of ages.

These remarks apply, not only to the candidates for
offices or emoluments under government, but to those who
are crowding themselves into the learned professions,
without those qualifications which ought to be considered
as indispensable.

I know that Duane and the Jacobins of his school,
maintain, that the learned professions, particularly that
of Law, ought to be annihilated ; and they may as well
be annihilated, as to be crowded with witlings and unqualified professors.   But it is to be hoped the good sense
of Americans will resist the innovations of these God-
winian schemers.

Duane and his faction, may as well declare against
watch-makers,. tailors, or any other mechanics, as law-
yers, or gentlemen of the other learned professions.—
They are each subservient to the happiness or convenience of all, and altogether constitute a civilized nation.
But if what we have advanced in our exposition of the
principles of Mr. Godwin, in Canto II. relative to the
tendency of these and similar levelling tenets, should.

No cobbler leave, at Faction's call,
His *last*, and thereby lose his *all*.

No brawny blacksmith, brave and stout,
Our Constitution *hammer* out,
For if he's wise, he'll not desire
Too many *irons* in the fire ;—

And though a master of his trade,
With politics on *anvil* laid,
He may take many a *heat*, and yet he
Can't *weld* a bye-law or a treaty.

No tailor, than his *goose* more silly,
Should cut the State a garment, till he
Is sure he has the *measure* right,
Lest it *fit* awkward, *loose* or *tight*.

make no impression on the reader, we must turn him over
to the demagogues of the day.

130 Should set himself to *patch* the state.

"When tinkers bawl'd aloud to settle
Church discipline, for patching kettle," &c.
HUDIBRAS, Part I. Canto II.

No farmer, had he Ceres' skill,
The commonwealth should think to *till*,
For many *soils* in human nature,
Would mock his art as *cultivator*.

The greatest number's greatest good,
Should, doubtless, ever be pursu'd ;
But that consists, *sans* disputation,
In order and subordination.

Nature imposes her commands,
There must be *heads*, as well as *hands*,131

131 There must be *heads*, as well as *hands*.

If our New School politicians are not too fastidious to peruse with patience, even the Apocryphal part of the Bible, we would beg leave to illustrate our ideas on this subject, by a quotation from Ecclesiasticus, Chapter XXXVIII. v. 24, to the end of the chapter.

" The wisdom of a learned man cometh by opportuni_ ty of leisure : and he that hath little business shall become wise.

" How can he get wisdom that holdeth the plough, and that glorieth in the goad; that driveth oxen, and is occupied in their labours, and whose talk is of bullocks?

The man of body, " son of soul,"
The former happiest on the whole :—132.

" He giveth his mind to make furrows ; and is diligent
to give the kine fodder.

" So every carpenter and workmaster that laboureth
night and day : and they that cut and grave seals, and
are diligent to make great variety, and give themselves to
counterfeit imagery, and watch to finish a work :

" The smith also sitting by the anvil, and considering
the iron work, the vapour of the fire wasteth his flesh,
and he fighteth with the heat of the furnace : the noise
of the hammer and the anvil is ever in his ears, and his
eyes look still upon the pattern of the thing that he maketh ; he setteth his mind to finish his work, and watcheth
to polish it perfectly :

" So doth the potter sitting at his work, and turning
the wheel about with his feet, who is always carefully set
at his work : and maketh all his work by number ;

" He fashioneth the clay with his arm, and bow-
eth down his strength before his feet, he applieth himself to lead it over ; and he is diligent to make clean the
furnace :

" All these trust to their hands : and every one is wise
in his work.

" Without these cannot a city be inhabited : and they
shall not dwell where they will, nor go up and down :
They shall not be sought for in public counsel, nor sit

For toil of body still we find,
Is lighter far than toil of mind,

high in the congregation: they shall not sit on the judges' seat, nor understand the sentence of judgment: they cannot declare jus.ice and judgment, and they shall not be found where parables are spoken.

" But they will maintain the state of the world, and [all] their desire is in the work of the craft."

It is impossible for any person who is truly a philan. thropist not to feel his indignation excited against the perverse philosophists of the day, who, instead of inculcating *patience* and *tranquillity* among mankind, are continually exciting that restive and turbulent spirit, which is the bane of civilized society. · It is owing to their efforts that the hearts of the lower classes in the community are so frequently " Cankered with discontent, that they consider themselves as condemned to labour for the luxury of the rich, and lcok up with stupid malevolence towards those who are placed above them."*

132 The former happiest on the whole :—

He who has been in early life accustomed to laborious occupations, can rarely conform to sedentary pursuits : accustomed to the *stimulus* of violent *corporeal exercise,*

---

* *Johnson's Rasselas, Prince of Abysinnia.*

And nought, perhaps, but tooth-ach pains,
Can equal " wear and tear of brains."

Blest is the man with wooden head,
Who labours for his daily bread,
More happy he, if truth were known,
Than Buonapart' upon his throne :—

Yes, his advantage most immense is,
In all enjoyments of the senses,
If health and strength in him are join'd,
With heaven's best boon, a tranquil mind.

Then think not Providence disgrac'd you,
If in some lower rank it plac'd you ;
Think poverty no punishment,
And be with competence content ;

his frame will be disordered, from its discontinuance.
Listlessness, apathy, hypochondriacal complaints, and
not unfrequently madness, swell the catalogue of disorders
which await a transition of that kind.   Hence the im-
practicability of civilizing the aborigines of America, who
have, in early life, been inured to the toil of the hunter
state.

Do not assume of State the reins,
If you're but so so, as to brains,
Because you make yourselves vexation,
And but disgrace us as a nation.

Had Johnny Randolph known his place,
He had not hunted Mr. CHASE,[133]
Nor had the public known him to be
A blundering and malicious booby.

133 He had not hunted Mr. CHASE.

The failure of this poor little " ghost of a monkey,"
in his impeachment of Mr. Chase, cannot but afford
high satisfaction to every friend to his country. We have
reason to believe that had Mr. Chase fallen, it was the
intention of the stripling tyrant, and his confederate
mamelukes, to have destroyed all the Federal Judges, at
" one fell swoop."

It was happily so ordered, that he made his attack on
one every way able to defend himself against the malicious and vindictive assaults of the Faction, and who has
not only repelled the shafts of their calumny, but by his
masterly vindication of his conduct, has done honour to
Federalism and to his country.

Had Lawyer L——n staid at home,
His honour might have pass'd, with some,
For quite a decent country Squire,
And no bad Jury—*argufier*.

And had our Governor that would be,
But been contented where he should be,
His Honour had not been the mark
So often hit by D—r P—k.[134]

Had——somebody but known his station,
Perhaps his blasted reputation,

134 So often hit by D—r P—k.

The charges to which we here allude, are already before the public. We offer no comments, but merely observe, that the man, who, after having witnessed the developement of the character of this candidate for the
Gubernatorial chair will give him his suffrage, has not
virtue enough to qualify him to be the citizen of a *free
government* ; and if a majority of the citizens of Massachusetts are base enough to prefer this man to Governor
Strong, national freedom is at its last gasp, and the character of the State is fast sinking to the lowest point of
degradation.

Stain'd by a multitude of sins,
Had 'scap'd the shafts of Young and Minns.
[135

So much for wiseacres, desiring
To show their folly by aspiring,
We turn to those who know their places,
And form our social fabric's basis.

I need not tell you, Sirs, how true 'tis,
That you have *rights*, as well as *duties*,
Have much at stake in preservation
Of Law and order in the nation.

135 Had 'scap'd the shafts of Young and Minns.

We allude here to the well known publication in the New-England Palladium, entitled, ". The monarchy of Federalism," which gives in short hand, a correct idea of the man whom our Democrats " *delight to honour.*" The pamphlet, entitled, " The Defence of Young and Minns," which contains copies of the documents, and statements of the facts alluded to in that publication, ought to be in the hands of every American freeman who is not disposed to rush blindfold into the jaws of destruction.

S

But heed you not the bawling clan,
Who prate about the " rights of man,"
Although like Thomas Pain, and Firm,
They fix no meaning to the term.[136]

See Elliot sick of the procedures[137]
Of our good Democratic leaders,

136 They fix no meaning to the term.

Nothing can be more preposterous than the declama-
tory nonsense of the demagogues of the day, who clamour
about the " rights of man."   If these gentlemen wish to
mix a little *knowledge* with their zeal on this subject, they
will diligently con Judge Blackstone's Commentaries, particularly the first Chapter of the first Book, which treats
of the " Rights of Persons."

137 See Elliot sick of the procedures.

'Mr. Elliot's letters to his constituents display very considerable candor, and certain aproximations to rectitude,
for which he ought to receive a due degree of credit.
   This gentleman, together with many others, much his
inferiors in abilities and integrity, was elected to Congress
by a party who were opposed to the Washington and
Adams administration ; but perceiving that the views of

Is *half* resolv'd on coming round,
And occupying Federal ground.

the leaders of that party were destructive to the Constitution, Laws and Liberty of the Union, he appears now to halt between two opinions. He will, by no means, acknowledge himself to be a Federalist, although his political tenets appear *now* to be very nearly the same with those *always* held by the Federal party. Perhaps, however, he may hereafter observe of some other political subjects what he has already remarked relative to a certain amendment of the Constitution, that he "had never contemplated the subject with a suitable degree of cool reflection and deep investigation."* No doubt a proper attention to con: templations of that kind might induce him to become *altogether* a Federalist !

We cannot, however, forbear to notice a slight inconsistency which appears in his "political creed," as expressed in his 11th letter to his constituents. Mr. Elliot says, "I believe that Washington was the greatest warrior and probably the most *correct statesman* in our country. I believe Adams to be a man of integrity and talents, but the general system of his Administration was wrong." Now a "correct statesman" is not apt to give his sanction to *wrong* measures, but Washington did highly approve of Mr. Adams' Administration, as appears by his letter to Mr. Carrol. See Vol. I. N. 145. P. 163.

---

* *See Mr. Elliot's 3d Letter to his Constituents.*

And others feel a foolish terror
'Gainst owning they have been in error,
And though convinc'd, are not so manly
As Butler, Elliot, and Stanley.[138]

Be not of good men over jealous,
Nor lightly trust the clamorous fellows,
Who 'gainst your true friends set their faces,
Merely to crowd into their places.

There must be limits put to suffrage,[139]
Although the step excite enough rage,

138 As Butler, Elliot, and Stanley.

These gentlemen have all been of the Democratic party, but had honesty and independence enough to oppose
the machinations of the Virginian junto.

139 There must be limits put to suffrage.

It cannot be necessary in this place, to repeat what
has been so often urged on the subject of " Universal
Suffrage." Some qualifications as respects property, re-
sidence, and citizenship, ever have, and ever will be
found necessary in a civilized state of society, in order to

Lest men devoid of information
And honesty should rule the nation.

Your multiplying institutions,
Checks, balances and constitutions,140
Which rogues can break down with im-
    punity,
Will serve no purpose in community.

entitle a man by his vote, to dispose of the property of
others. What should we say of one, who assumed a
right to direct the operations, and tax the shares of a
private company of merchants, who held no stock belonging to the company?

140 Checks, balances and constitutions.

In that invaluable digest of the principles of our government entitled " The Federalist" we find the following
apprehensions expressed on this subject.

" Experience assures us that the efficacy of *parch-
ment barriers* has been greatly over-rated, and that some
more adequate defence is indispensably necessary, for the
more feeble against the more powerful members of the
government. The Legislative department is every where

S 2

Thus Despotism France controuls,
In spite of Sieyes' pigeon holes, ·
And Revolutions every Moon,
Could not secure her Freedom's boon.

Let honesty and reputation,
Be passports to your approbation,
And ne'er support, with zeal most hearty,
A knave because he's of your party.

Remember, mid your party strife,
Whoso's a rogue in *private life*,[141]

extending the sphere of its activity, and drawing all power into its impetuous vortex·"*

If this " more *adequate defence*" should not be found in *public opinion*, our Constitution will fall, our political and civil rights will soon share its fate, and despotism in America, as in France, will at length prove our only *asylum* from the horrors of anarchy.

141 Whoso's a rogue in *private life*.

One of the most dangerous errors of those among our democrats, who are rather the *deluded* than the *deluders*, is an

---

* *The remarks of the eloquent Mallet Du Pan, on the fate of Switzerland, corroborate these observations.*

If once.he gets you at his beck
Will set his foot upon your neck.

Thus Mr: Burr, for aye intriguing,,
With this side, and with that side leaguing,
Has late contriv'd a scheme quite handy,
To make himself, for life, a grandee.142

opinion that our attention to the affairs of government
ought to be directed altogether to *measures* without adverting to *men*. But an *evil tree* cannot produce *good fruit*,
neither can ignorant wrongheaded and wicked men give
origin and support to measures which are beneficial to the
public. Yet how often do we trust those in *public station*
in whom we could place no confidence in *private life*,
and how many democrats like Matthew Lyon give
countenance to your Duanes and Cheethams, knowing
them such as Lyon has described his "old friend," that
is entirely destitute of common honesty. Such men deserve to be made "hewers of wood and drawers of water,"
as a punishment for their stupidity, lack of political
honesty, and public spirit.

142 To make himself, for life, a grandee.

Mr. Burr's attempt to obtain the privilege of franking
letters is an indication of the kind of freedom with which

You next some method must be trying,
To stop the rage of party lying,
Which may be quickly done, provided
You will be honest and decided,

When printers are to lies addicted,
And have most fairly been convicted;
For instance, men like Chronicleers,
Who should be thankful—for their ears.

From pillory though they are exempt,
You ought to blast them with contempt,
But now they find, by Faction's aid,
Lying a profitable trade.

But you can stop our Demo's dashing,
Bring honesty again in fashion,
Bring scoundrelism to disgrace,
Bid modest merit show its face.

he and his party would favour the simpletons, who are ca-
pahle of being lulled to repose by the syren song of Liberty and Equality.

Instead of sinking in despair,
Be as with WASHINGTON you *were,*
Revive the measures he approv'd,
RESTORE TO POWER THE MEN HE LOV'D ! 143

143 RESTORE TO POWER THE MEN HE LOV'D.

Those men who were honoured with the confidence of their fellow-citizens and appointed to office under Washington and Adams' Administration, were selected from among their fellow-citizens, because they were known to be " honest and faithful." Now the inquiry, as Mr. J——n's answer to the New-Haven remonstrance implies, is altogether whether the candidate is of the right political sect. The demon of party brought forward the Democrats, not any intrinsic merits of their own. The same evil spirit which gave France her Marats, her Roberspieres, and her Buonaparte, has given America the tyrants who have put a period to the political existence of the Federalists, and who, as Duane has intimated, would lead them to the scaffold if they dared. If we have not virtue enough to retrace our steps and return to primitive men and measures, we may foresee in the fall of France what must be the termination of our struggles for Liberty.

Then may you rationally hope
That *Liberty*, without a trope,
And all the virtues of her train,
Will deign to visit us again.144

144 Will deign to visit us again.

Many of our luke-warm Federalists, seem disposed to
slide down the steep of Democracy, without an effort to
save themselves and country, from the *unlimited misery*
which awaits such a career.   They say, that Americans
have not *virtue* enough to support a Republican Government, and that we had better remain contented under the
present state of our affairs, than by exertions which must
prove fruitless, to hazard the introduction of a still worse
order of things.   But this is very foolish reasoning.   As
well might a physician determine to give no medicine to
allay the rage of a fever, because the disorder *will have
its crisis*.   If the efforts of the Federalists should be un-
remitted, they will be, at least, able to muzzle the Mammoth of Democracy, and evade much of the evil which
would inevitably ensue, should the monster be suffered to
roam perfectly unrestrained.   But we cannot better conclude this note, than with the remarks of the Editor of
the Utica Patriot, an excellent Federal Newspaper.

   " The cause of Federalism, we trust, has passed its
most gloomy period.   The *ebb tide* has arrived to its utmost point, and will shortly be succeeded by a flood,

But, my good sovereign friends, I now
Must make, alas, my parting bow,
Still humbly hoping, with submission,
That you'll attend to my Monition.

Take my advice, which not pursuing,
You're surely in the " road to ruin,"
For rul'd by men, and not by law,
Your rights will not be worth a straw.

which will overwhelm its enemies in one prodigious ruin.
The government again in the hands of the Federalists,
the wounds which have been inflicted on the constitution,
would be shortly healed, the government would conva-
lesce from its present weakness, to perfect health and vigour, and the blessings of rational liberty would again be
enjoyed in their pristine purity. Then let Federalists,
knowing the justice of their cause, and its importance to
the salvation of their country, be animated to exertion;
and let each good man and true patriot adopt for himself, the language of the Poet:

——" Here I take my stand,
Here on the brink, the very verge of liberty :
Although contention rise upon the clouds,
Mix heaven with earth, and roll the ruin onwards,
Here will I fix, and breast me to the shock,
TILL I OR DENMARK FALL."

FINIS.

EXTRACTS FROM REVIEWS

OF

Democracy Unveiled,

AND.

OTHER PUBLICATIONS OF THE SAME AUTHOR.

—

" WHOEVER reads Democracy Unveiled with candour, even if his muscles be distorted with anguish by the castigation so liberally bestowed on the rulers of the most numerous party in 'this country, will' readily credit the assertion of the author, that " personal animosity is not among the motives, which produced this poem." Though the smart of the culprit, under the beadle's lash, be little alleviated by the knowledge that his demerits have long required this exertion of Justice; yet the public will remember, that the punishment is not inflicted through wantonness, nor aggravated by malice.

The Poet, in his commencement, says,

> I would not wantonly annoy,—
> Would no one's happiness destroy;
> None lives, I say, with honest pride, who
> Despises slander more than I do.

And next assigns the reason of his satire,

T

I'll lash each knave that's now in vogue,
Meiely because he is a rogue.

"Democracy Unveiled should be read by every person in the community, especially by the
middling classes of citizens, for whom it seems
chiefly intended."

*The Monthly Anthology, and Boston
Review, for July,* 1805.

....

EXTRACTS FROM ENGLISH REVIEWS OF FOR-
MER PUBLICATIONS BY THE AUTHOR OF DE-
MOCRACY UNVEILED.

" Terrible Tractoration, a poetical petition
against Galvanising Trumpery, and the Perkinistic Institution," &c....1st edition.

" These Hudibrastic lines have afforded us
amusement. It is not too much to say, that
the author is a legitimate branch of the Hudibras family, and possesses a vein of humour
which will not be easily exhausted."

Literary Journal, for September, 1803.

After stating how far inferior to Hudibras are
the generality of modern imitators, the Reviewers proceed, " To a charge of this nature
the author of the present poem pleads not
guilty. With the mantle of Butler he has likewise something of his inspiration, and has imitated him no less in his versification than in
the spirit which supports it."

Monthly Register Review, for May, 1803.

. " The author deals his blows around with such causticity, sparing neither friend nor foe, from the "indelible ink" of Dr. Lettsom, and the kindred " jangle of Matilda's lyre" to Dr. Darwin, tracing organised molecules from slaughtered armies to tribes of insects, and thence again to nobler animals, through the profoundest parts of the *bathos*, and the sublimest of the *hupsos*, that his real object cannot be always ascertained. We think him, however, the friend of the Tractors, and peculiarly severe on Dr. Haygarth and Dr. Lettsom. Our author's knowledge seems to be extensive ; and he is by no means sparing of his communications. His descriptions are animated and poetical."

Critical Review, for November, 1803.

" We must acknowledge that this poem has a considerable share of Hudibrastic drollery. The author is particularly happy in his ludicrous compounded rhymes, and has many other qualities to ensure no trifling success in doggrel verse." After a quotation from the work, the Reviewers again mention its " ingenious burlesque," and " humorous. notes."

British Critic, for May, 1808.

" These four Cantos of Hudibrastic verse, and the copious notes, contain much pointed satire and sarcastic animadversion, in the form and guise of ironical compliments, on the medical opposers of the Metallic Tractors."

After a quotation from the work, they continue...."The attack on some of the cruel and indecent experiments of certain modern naturalists, which seem limited to the gratification of a licentious curiosity, having for their object the production of no one possible practical good, is just and commendable: and indeed the author has not merely rhyme but frequently reason on his side."

Anti-Jacobin Review, for April, 1803.

"In the first Canto, the author, in an inimitable strain of irony, ridicules those pretended discoveries and inventions of certain pseudophilosophers, both of the natural and moral class, which have no tendency to meliorate the condition of man." After many extracts from the work, and similar encomiums on each of the four Cantos, the Reviewers conclude.... "Whatever may be the merits of the Metallic Tractors, or the demerits of their opponents, we have no hesitation to pronounce this performance to be far superior to the ephemeral productions of ordinary dealers in rhymes. The notes, which constitute more than half the book, are not behind the verse in spirit. Who the author can be, we have not the least conception, but from the intimate acquaintance he discovers with the different branches of medical science, we should imagine him to be some jolly son of Galen, who not choosing to bestow all his art upon his PATIENTS, has humanely applied a few ESCHAROTICS for the benefit of his brethren."

Gentleman's Magazine for January, 1804.

The following are extracted from such Reviews of the second London edition of Terrible Tractoration as have fallen within our notice.

" For a general character of this ingenious and truly humorous poem, we must refer our reader to Vol. XIV. of our Review. The present edition is not merely a re-print of. the former, but contains more than double the quantity of matter; and to its increased bulk its value bears a due proportion."

" The ludicrous animadversion on the gossamery theories of the philosophistic Darwin, now forming a part of the third Canto, is entitled to praise; and though the extract is somewhat longer than we could wish, we are confident that our readers will derive much gratification from perusing it." The Reviewers conclude this article by a quotation of several pages from the third canto of the poem.

Anti-Jacobin Review, for August, 1804.

" In the second edition of this work the object of the author is more conspicuous: indeed it blazes with a lustre which leaves not the smallest foundation for doubt; and not confining himself to the Tractors, he aims his blows at many absurdities in the philosophy of medicine. Such, in fact, there are, and ridicule is, perhaps, the only weapon with which they can be attacked. Our author applies his flagellation with no sparing hand."

Critical Review, for January, 1804.

T. 2

EXTRACTS FROM AMERICAN REVIEWS OF TERRI-
BLE TRACTORATION.

" The satire and irony of the burlesque part
(of Terrible Tractoration) are not employed
solely against the enemies of the Perkinistic
Institution, which it is his principal object to defend. In his excursive flight of poetry, and in
the well written and amusing notes to his merry cantos, he has very successfully ridiculed many of the disciples of the *new school*, who,
either by jacobin politics, or atheistical philosophy, or perverted literature, have attempted to
disturb the peace, and deface the felicity of
mankind. The author, whom we know to be
a disciple of the Old School, and who has always proved himself an anti-gallican, anti-jaco-
binical and anti-fanatical partizan, has acquitted
himself with great ability in that part of his
work which is occupied in satirising the upstart
innovators of the time." " We hope that the
well principled wit, who has so severely lashed
the foolish and the flagitious in the Old World,
will brandish his scourge against the culprits of
the New."

The Port Folio, for August 18, 1804.

" This is a humorous poem, in which the stile
of Hudibras is most happily imitated. Those
who delight to laugh at the philosophic follies of
the day, will be much gratified by the perusal of
" Terrible Tractoration." In every age the
half-learned are offering their wild theories, and

exhibiting their minute discoveries to the world, for which they claim high seats in the Temple of Science, and demand ever-green honours. Such always find gazers to look up and admire, whilst flattery decorates them with laurels. It is the part of satire to assign them their proper rank, and to strip from their brows the unmerited wreaths, which encompass them. To a certain portion of the philosophists and empyrics of the day, Christopher Caustic has performed this office.

Monthly Anthology and Boston Review, for February, 1805.

" In commending CHRISTOPHER CAUSTIC, we are only subscribing to the opinions expressed by the people of another country. To be behind that country, in our appreciation, of his merits, were a stigma ; it is very pardonable to go beyond it. National vanity may be a folly, but national ingratitude is a crime. Terrible Tractoration was successful on its first appearance in England, and as yet seems to have lost none of its popularity. It belongs to that class of productions, which have the good fortune to escape what Johnson angrily, but too justly, denominates the general conspiracy of human nature against cotemporary merit."

The Monthly Anthology, for April, 1805.

EXTRACTS FROM ENGLISH REVIEWS OF "ORIGI-
NAL POEMS, BY THE AUTHOR OF "DEMO-
CRACY UNVEILED."

" A vein of pleasantry and sportive humour
is manifested by this American writer, which
cannot fail to amuse and conciliate the reader,
when he is disposed to quit his serious studies
and welcome a playful guest." " Whenever an
opportunity occurs, the author takes care to in-
culcate in the minds of his countrymen a spirit
of manly independence, and a rational love of
liberty." The Reviewers then make a quotation from the work, and conclude as follows :

" We recommend these patriotic lines to the
attention of our own countrymen, as worthy of
a great and independent nation. In the mean-
time, we are happy to observe that this author
expresses his wishes to preserve and perpetuate
harmony between his country and England.
We trust and hope that such a disposition is
cordially cherished by the freeborn inhabitants
of both states."

Monthly Review.

" We were amused with the burlesque poem,
called " Terrible Tractoration." That Mr. F.
possesses a singular genius for burlesque poetry
is undeniable, and is rendered still more evident
by the present volume.

" But there is another circumstance which,
strongly recommends these poems to notice.
They present a new literary phenomenon ; a

poetical miscellany written by an American author; and what is still more pleasing to us, an American friendly to England and to genuine liberty."

" Of the author's humour, we might produce as specimens, his burlesque Sapphics, in the stile of the famous " Needy Knife Grinder."— The Vermont Pastoral is in a new stile, and very illustrative of local manners ; the allusions to which give an air of novelty to every part of the volume. Mr. Fessenden is seldom more successful than when he is satirizing the profligate democrats of America. His poems have afforded us much gratification."

British Critic.

" We presume this writer to be an American ; and, considering the state of literature in that country, his productions are quite as good as could be expected from one of its natives. His serious productions are, upon the whole, the best ; still he is, by no means, destitute of humour."

Critical Review.

" In a well written preface to this volume of poems, Mr. Fessenden makes some judicious remarks on the growing importance of America, in the scale of nations.

" The major part of these poems are humorous, and are principally worthy of attention for their accurate delineation of rustic manners in New-England. The patriotic ode, at the beginning of the volume has much merit; and the serious pieces that are inserted, afford a favourable specimen of the author's poetical talents, as well as of his political and moral principles."

Anti-Jacobin Review.

Errata,

IN THE FIRST VOLUME.

Page 25, lines 5 and 6 from the top, for "*additional notes at the end of the volume*," read *following notes in this volume.*

Page 35, line 6 from the bottom, before "*whom*" insert *to.*

Page 53, line 15 from the bottom, Greek word, for "*Pantogrator*," read *Pantokrator.*

Page 98, line 3 from the bottom, for "*Edwin*," read *Eusden.*

Page 104, line 3 from the bottom, for "*mouldering*," read *smouldering.*

Page 122, line 2 from the bottom, dele "CHURCHILL."

Page 126, line 4 from the bottom, for "*led to that step*," read *was laid.*

Page 159, line 10 from the top, for "*hid*," read *did.*

IN THE SECOND VOLUME.

Page 19, line 5 from the top, for "*comica*," read *comical.*

Page 68, line 4 from the bottom, for "*Mareat*," read *moveat.*

Index

OF PERSONS MENTIONED IN DEMOCRACY UNVEILED.

N. B. The first figures denote the Volumes and the following the pages.

A

Adams,	I. 45, 127, 130, 149.—II. 60, 67, 71, [143, 144, 145
Absalom,	I. 123
Abner,	I. 125
Ægis-man,	I. 11
Æneas,	II. 182
Addison,	I. 6
Amar,	I. 64
Ames,	I. 179
Arcularius,	II. 169, 170

B

Babcock,	II. 22, 25

U

C

D

INDEX.

G.

H.

U 2

J

K

L

In some few copies the following ERRATA, *in the Preface and Introduction, escaped notice.*

Page vi, line 21 from the top, for " ins," read *complains.*

Page viii, line 17 from the top, for " scourge," read *lash.*

Lightning Source UK Ltd.
Milton Keynes UK
UKHW022232140219
337291UK00006B/165/P